BOXEDMAN

I'm Going To Make A Movie, Why Are You Laughing?

NICHOLAS PASYANOS

Published 2021 by Next Chapter

Edited by India Hammond

Large Print Edition

Contents

Forward v

1. How It Started 1
2. Jim Cameron And Stephen Spielberg Come To Town 10
3. Help In Casting 25
4. First Day Of Shooting 53
5. Ace Is Back 61
6. Porn Shop Shoot 68
7. The Antagonist Is Ready 76
8. The Nose Picker Is Found 81
9. Life Imitates Art Or Vice Versa 86
10. Drinking Beers At 10 Am 93
11. Billie Price Being Billie Price 98
12. Snow In Summer 104
13. A Frustrating Night Scene 109
14. I Break My Friend's Car Window 114
15. The Bottling Plant 122
16. Bjs, Limos, And Cops 129
17. My Movie Comes To Life As Titanic Sails Into History 133
18. Ten Degree Beach Day 141
19. Theater Reshoot And Clean Up 147
20. Four Months Of Editing 152

21. A Composer That Gets It 156
22. Post Master Sound 162
23. Film Festival Debut 165
24. Close But No Cigar 185
25. The Screenplay 193
Images 437

Dear Reader 463

Forward

FIRST TIME FILM MAKERS ODYSSEY

So, you want to know what it's like to make your first movie when you have no formal training or experience? This is a good place to start. Best of all, you'll experience it from the perspective of someone who didn't create a "Blair Witch" phenomenon, but a typical, truly independent film that got lost in the sea of other films seeking a distributor or home of some sort.

It was truly a Herculean effort both physically and financially to shoot on film and edit digitally. At the time, one out of every twenty films landed a home. Mine was not one of them. Since then, the rise of digital film making, editing, and web access has made this opportunity easier and cheaper than ever to execute. If you have a voice in your head saying, "I think I can make a movie and hopefully get discovered," don't ignore it. Living with regrets is something I highly recommend avoiding.

There are many successful film makers that have written "How-To Books," which could influence you to think, "Hey, I can do that too." The reality is much like what happens in any casino, there are a few big winners and a lot more losers. This book will enlighten you to the challenges and realities of making a feature length film on the cheap. I attempted to show all sides of the experience so that you can appreciate what lies ahead. If, after you read this, your inner muse is still saying go, I'd say go. In the chapters to follow, I will attempt to clearly delineate my thoughts, whether philosophical, opinion, fact, absolute fact, superstition, or neurotic self-doubt. In this way, you can get the most from my experience.

Best of luck.

1

How It Started

I'M GONNA MAKE A MOVIE! I announced with great trepidation to the circle of casual friends gathered around me in the cockpit of my sailboat. Possibly a nanosecond passed before my friend, Ron, broke out laughing so hard I thought he might suffer internal injuries. Ron, you see, is a well-grounded, self-made entrepreneur who owns successful businesses in several states. Constant travel between businesses, homes, and worldwide vacations, keeps him and his wife in perpetual motion. Ron has what many would consider an enviable life.

The occasion was our annual get together sail with Ron and his wife Sandy, another couple of Ron's friends, and my girlfriend Carol, who sat silently observing this exchange. Carol, knowing of my commitment to the project, was the only one not laughing at what the others saw as my apparent loss of mind. She was also the only one to know that I was quickly becoming a best customer of Border's, Barnes & Noble, and independent bookstores everywhere. I was consuming filmmaking books at a book a week pace. This was my approach to an ambitious, self-paced, educational process to ready myself to make the film.

Ron proceeded to fire questions at me, questions that were unavoidably important to a businessman evaluating a project. His questions were sensible. 1) Will you be taking time off from work? 2) Do you have adequate financing? 3) Do you have experienced help?

My answers were 1) "NO," I can't leave my job, because I need the money. 2) "NO," I have to personally fund the project because it would be too hard a sell, to find investors, given the circumstances. 3) "NO" again, because I don't know anyone that has any film making experience. This was why I'd given myself a year to educate and prepare for the film I'd planned to start shooting in the summer of 1997. The year would also allow me time to purchase all the equipment, find shooting locations, and cast the film. I saw no point in going into the overwhelming fact that I had 60 shooting locations and 43 speaking roles to fill. Why offer up ammunition to be shot with?

The more I tried explaining myself to this logical businessman, the further I got from convincing him how serious I was. He was thinking that if this was a business venture, he didn't feel good about it. Futility prevailed, I threw in the towel, and shut up. Ron's continued chuckling over the next couple hours as we plied the waves fortified my resolve and convinced me not to talk about my project to any thinking, sane, person again.

First off, I need to relate some personal history so that you can try to understand my apparent insanity and passion. I have always been a film buff. I have had a love affair with movies my entire life. From adolescence, I had seen way more movies than any of my friends. I was born in Boston, and my family lived two blocks from Fenway Park for the first seven years of my life. After my first seven years, we moved every couple of years, but not more than a few miles from the former residence.

Today, we have multiplexes that have most of the current releases playing under one roof. Back then, in the 50's and 60's, theaters only exhibited a double feature. The main movie was coupled with a second, lesser film, kind of like an A side and a B side on an old 45 RPM vinyl record, if you're old enough to get that reference (if not, Google/Wikipedia). You had to search the newspapers to find the movie you wanted to see and hope it was nearby. Between downtown Boston and the immediate suburbs, there were countless theaters with an impressive range available to us. On Washington Street, in downtown Boston, there was the Paramount, the RKO, and Cinerama. All of them were very large venues by today's standard.

Cinerama is a format that, due to its production and exhibition costs, is extinct and will never be seen again. Cinerama was unique because the screen was narrow, top to bottom, and proportionately very long, left to right, 90 feet long to be exact. The fact that the screen was very long, and had a curve in it, filling your peripheral vision, created the feel that you were immersed in the image. Today that aspect ratio would be stated as 2:55 to 1 or could be as wide as 2:78 to 1. Most films today are shot 1:85 to 1, or 2:35 to 1. The narrow and long image was possible because movies made for Cinerama was shot with a specially built camera with three lenses shooting left, center, and right. The three cameras filmed every scene simultaneously. When the film was projected in the theater, they used three projectors with the same spacing. The projected images overlapped in a seamless fashion, creating this panoramic view. Beautiful to look at, but all costs are now more than tripled. Is it any surprise that when Hollywood hit cost conscious times, Cinerama disappeared? Fortunately, several of the movies that I saw there are out in DVD now. Check them out and see just how wide they are. Some of the titles are: *It's a Mad, Mad, Mad, Mad World, Beyond the 12 Mile Reef, How the West Was Won, Grand Prix,* and *The Wonderful World of the Brothers Grimm.*

One other theater worth mentioning still exists: the Brattle Cinema in Harvard Square. It was and still is an art house theater, although at the time I wasn't aware of that distinction, nor, frankly, would I have known what that meant. It was where I saw subtitled foreign films and little-known movies, like *Lord of the Flies,* which didn't play at the other theaters. Although my sister and I had exposure to a diverse range of movies, as with most kids, we preferred standard popcorn matinee fare.

Every summer we got a mega-dose of movies because of my father's occupation. A chef in Boston restaurants, my father took a sabbatical every summer to run restaurants on Cape Cod. That transplanted our family for the entire summer to a number of seaside towns. My sister Irene (who is four years younger than I) and I were in the same boat. We didn't know the local kids, so we became sole companions to each other. The local movie theaters became our other companion. The theaters in these communities changed movies every two-to-three days, probably because they were attempting to get viewers to visit twice if they were on a one-week vacation. Guess who got to see every movie that was released those summers? Right! And we didn't even miss the ones that didn't interest us. We no doubt became their best customers, but I'm not so sure they appreciated our patronage. My sister and I, coming from a family in the restaurant business, were very adventurous eaters. We used to bring our own munchies to the theater. Odd things like pistachio nuts, canned sardines, and canned anchovies. Only now can I imagine the cleaning crew at the end of the night discovering pistachio nut shells and empty tins of olive oil under the seats we sat in. No one ever confronted us, probably because we were some of their best patrons. Those were memorable summers, for both us and the theater owners. But the biggest reason we saw so many movies during the rest of the year was because my mother used the theaters as our babysitter. Our mother would take us to the theater, get us seated, armed with hours' worth of eats. She would return later to pick us up after she'd finished her errands or shopping. (This was back when child abduction wasn't a concern.)

As I mentioned earlier, all shows included two films that alternated continuously. Sometimes we wouldn't get to see the second film in its entirety and other times we got to see both movies once or twice. The repeat viewing was when I would get the opportunity to dissect the film. I was studying the structure and assembly of the movie subconsciously. Little did I know it but that was the start of my filmmaking education; an education that I wouldn't put into action until over thirty years later. During those years, I graduated high school, got married, got divorced, and worked for a living (CliffsNotes version). Basically, life got in the way, and frequent visits to the theater wasn't part of it. During those years, most of my movie viewing was on network TV's movie of the week. Movies would be shown on TV only after several years had passed from their release date, and you'd have to endure what felt like endless commercial breaks. A two-hour movie would be broken up with an hour of commercials. It was considered an EVENT when a movie was shown within a year and a half of its theatrical release date. An amusing far cry from today's video, cable, satellite services, and streaming that offer vast content within months of their theatrical release. Without a doubt, the most significant development in my life of movie viewing had to be the advent of the home video formats of videotape and laserdiscs. Sometime in the mid 80's, VCR machine prices dropped to an affordable level, and video rental shops started opening all over town. As America adopted the new technology, I resumed my voracious pursuit of movie viewing. Video afforded me the opportunity to get caught up on all the movies I had missed. It was only natural for me to start collecting video cassettes of my favorite films. I collected video cassettes for approximately six years until I discovered the next best thing. The laserdisc.

My introduction to the laserdisc came by way of a plug from the then Siskel and Ebert movie review TV show. The format had been around for close to a decade, but was not mainstream. It was the format that only serious movie buffs and filmmakers watched and collected. Siskel and Ebert were both laserdisc collectors, which basically turned me into one. The advantages of the format were a sharper picture, more accurate color, and correct framing (widescreen vs. the compromised full screen format that broadcast TV and video cassettes had).

The best part of all was the alternate audio track that contained the director's commentary. This is a feature that is very common on today's DVDs but was an exclusive perk on some laserdiscs. I purchased almost all the discs that had director's commentary tracks. I clearly got the filmmaking bug listening to them. The creative process of filmmaking really appealed to me. At that point in time, I had been a part-time portrait and wedding photographer for over 25 years. Photography and filmmaking were so closely related that I began to question the career paths I had taken in my life. I was now a 45-year-old, middle-aged guy with regrets and some deep-rooted questions emerging. Is what I'm feeling genuine regret, or some male menopause, mid-life crisis? My gut tells me it's regret.

2

Jim Cameron And Stephen Spielberg Come To Town

In the winter of 1994, Jim Cameron (director) was shooting the opening scenes of his film *True Lies* in Newport, RI, at Salve Regina College. I live only three miles from the campus.

Jim Cameron was one of my favorite directors, having made *The Abyss, Aliens, Terminator,* and *Terminator 2.* After *True Lies,* he made *Titanic* in 1997, which to this day is the second biggest box office hit in history, due to his *Avatar* taking the number one spot. Jim's coming to town to direct a movie with Arnold Schwarzenegger was all I needed to know.

Fortunately, my uncle Duke was the assistant deputy of security at the school. I asked if I could come and observe the filming.

"That would be difficult," he answered. "But I

have to hire a lot of people for security. I could get you a job in security for the eight days of filming. You can watch while on duty and get paid for it."

Well, if that didn't turn out to be the best part-time job of my life. For me, an aspiring filmmaker, it was Fantasy Camp. My work assignment was to prevent others from getting close to the filming. Strangely, there was a net of Newport Police officers outside our perimeter that prevented anyone from reaching us. So here I was securing nothing, watching a major motion picture being made by a famous director, eating free food along with the rest of the production staff, while earning $12 an hour doing it. I'm now understanding why major films cost so much to make.

No complaints from me. I was stationed very close to almost all the primary filming. I got to look over Jim Cameron's shoulders as he directed most of what is now the opening eight minutes of the movie. All the filming took place on freezing cold nights in February. The location was supposed to be in the Swiss Alps in winter, and it sure looked the part. John Bruno (the visual effects supervisor) took the images of Salve Regina's mansion administration building and digitally composited it into the images he had taken of the Alps. That winter was a severe one with snow falling every few days. In spite of Mother Nature's cooperating with the intended scenario, Jim

Cameron still felt it necessary to bring in a snow making truck to dress up the natural snow. This had something to do with the color of the snow. Clearly, nature knows nothing about color balance and realism. The snow making truck pretty much absorbed all the capacity of the Newport Ice Company. Tons of ice was delivered and fed into the snowmaking truck as fast as the deliveries were made, round the clock. The man-made snow was used for ground cover. All the windowsills of the mansion were adorned with a white, pad-like material wired on to assimilate snow on the sills. All this was installed with a rented cherry picker.

I'm not convinced that the average moviegoer would pick up on these details, but they sure didn't escape the attention of Jim Cameron, arguably the most detail-focused director in the industry. I was so excited to be a part of this whole thing that I was willing to make the personal compromises in my life. As the scenes in the movie took place at night, I had to do an eight day with little sleep marathon. I couldn't take time off from work, so I was working my day job and then showing up to work the night shift on the set. Getting very little sleep for eight straight days was never an issue given this incredible opportunity. I was too pumped up to get tired.

My *True Lies* experience was all the inspiration I needed. Then and there I knew that I had to find a way into the industry. The most accessible way, both logistically and expediently, was screenwriting. Screenwriting was the most logical entry point because it is the foundation upon which all movies stand. I would pursue this challenge fully aware of the odds of my ever getting anyone in Hollywood to read whatever it was I was going to write. Damning the odds, I forged ahead and purchased several books on screenwriting.

The first script I wrote after absorbing the basics was *Armageddon*. Not *the Armageddon* but my *Armageddon*. It is best described as a script that starts out as a conventional doomsday drama and ends with a science fiction/theological twist. I was so confident in my ability to pitch its marketability that it now permanently resides in my closet.

It's said that you should write about what you know, so the second script I wrote was *BOXedMAN*, the story of an insecure corrugated box salesman working for the boss from hell as he attempts to succeed in a business climate made up of either ambivalent or eccentric characters. Drawing upon countless selling situations I've encountered, the people involved, and combining a dose of humor from my comedic personality, made the script a natural to write.

The protagonist was an underdog guy, like me, who enters a business because he thinks he can make a lot of money, like me, looking for love, like me, working for a psycho, like me, and navigating a world of interesting characters...like me. My real-life job situation was consuming my subconscious to the point of fueling my writing. I was frustratingly employed as a sales rep by one of the world's largest box companies. The company was in financial trouble for several years, being helmed by a megalomaniac, with a staff of yes-men lackeys. They, as a group, drove the sales force, of which I was a part of, to the brink of servile resignation. The demands put on all sales reps coupled with the impossible situations they created between us and our customers were close to unbearable. We were beat, mentally, with no relief in sight.

Combine this impossible situation with the hopelessness that comes when working for a huge corporation and you can see the genesis of Scott Adams' *Dilbert* cartoon. If you don't work for a large corporation, read a couple *Dilberts* in your Sunday paper and I need not say more. As bad as all this sounds, I've got one more layer of frosting for this cake. The general manager, my immediate boss at my plant location, was not a nice guy. Many of my coworkers had the same opinion. We saw him as moody, mean spirited, and distrusting. Aside from that, I guess he was a good manager.

Living and working day after day in this environment was extremely hard. I started sleeping with a mouth guard which prevented me from waking in the morning with a mouth full of ivory dust. While I may have been keeping all this inside, emotionally, it was all imbedding itself in my subconscious and ultimately into my spec script. I could not, not write about this. Yet, while I was in the process of writing the script, it never occurred to me once that this was a cathartic, therapeutic experience. I knew consciously that my boss was going to be the antagonist in this story, but I failed to recognize that this was also a way for me to deal with his oppressive ways. So, my boss became the model for the antagonist in my film, which made me the natural model for the protagonist. Makes total sense, right?

The only other ingredient to this brew that would become a screenplay was the inspiration of two relatable films. *Working Girl* and *Tin Men* were both films about business, love, and bad bosses. I studied them and tried to capture some of their strong points.

BOXedMAN had taken over a year to write, including subsequent drafts. I learned later that nothing is ever final. You still make changes throughout rehearsals and actual filming. Call it perpetual evolution. All in all it was now completed and I was ready to start pitching it to whoever would listen. A trip to the bookstores resulted in a stack of books listing how to pitch, along with directories of agents, producers, and studios. But before I would send my first letter or make my first call, two consecutive events altered my track.

One night, I watched a video by another one of the successful new filmmakers of the 90's. I watched Edward Burn's first film effort *Brothers McMullen*. I was impressed and inspired by this well-made, small budget film. It had won best picture honors at the Sundance Film Festival in Park City, Utah the year before. My attraction to it increased after reading all the buzz surrounding it. Edward shot this film using his mother's home, borrowed apartments, and guerrilla style shooting in public places, which would avoid the hassle and expense of getting permits from municipalities. He shot it with a handful of actors and friends over seven months of weekends. He personally funded the project to the tune of $25,000. You see where I'm going here. I'm making connections. I'm starting to head down the slope without being sure I want to. The final push down the slope came the next morning.

I finished reading the last chapter in Robert Rodriguez book, *Rebel Without a Crew*. Robert is another one of the new filmmakers who broke out in the 90's. He made a low budget or should I say micro budget feature for $7,000 entitled *El Mari-*

achi. The extraordinary thing about *El Mariachi* is that it is an action film. Just about an impossibility when viewed through the prism of conventional wisdom. The other interesting fact surrounding this film was that he wrote the script while living in a test lab that he volunteered to be in for thirty days, which earned him $3,000, about half the film's production cost. You can't make this stuff up. Robert went on to be a studio player and write his memoirs, *Rebel Without a Crew*. The last chapter is entitled "10 Minute Film School," in which he advocates taking the bull by the horns and making your film as he had done. Be 'self-sufficient' and be scary as he oversimplifies the immense task. I buy this pitch, hook, line, and sinker as I follow my ambitions blindly.

The wheels start to turn. I am a portrait photographer. I can light a scene. I have good credit and low debt. I could buy a used camera, lights, and the film needed. My mind is crunching the possibilities. I have a script. I weigh that my story is similar to *Brothers McMullen* in the fact that there aren't any costly effects. That was made for $25,000. *El Mariachi* was made for $7,000. Bang! Fusion! *Brothers McMullen* and *El Mariachi* in a combustible reaction, yielding a moment of clarity for me. Some might think it was a moment of madness.

"I'm going to make my film *BOXedMAN*."

Do I have any other options? Sure, I can pitch my script to a bunch of people who won't take my calls.

"I'm *definitely* going to make *BOXedMAN*."

I hurriedly called Carol to tell her about my out-of-left-field decision. There's silence at her end as she absorbs what I just said. Having read the script, she's trying to envision what I'm saying.

"There are so many characters. There are so many locations. What, Where, Who, Why, How?" She continued firing off the most immediate obstacles she could think of. There are a lot of them.

"I'll figure it out," I countered. As I spend a good portion of my workday driving around visiting customers, I suspect she thinks I just drove off the highway into a bridge abutment. I tell her I'm okay and that I'm going to start planning for my production. Okay, she answers. I think she's humoring me.

That evening, I started my serious relationship with every bookstore in a 100 mile radius. Beginning then and for the next year, I'd pop into bookstores during my daily business travels and peruse the racks for new titles. I'd look for any books that I hadn't seen before, but thought would be beneficial. My focus was on any book that would simulate a film school curriculum. I needed to buy books on every aspect of filmmaking because I knew nothing. Filmmaking is a collaborative art where a group of experts band together for a period of time to produce a finished product. My job was to learn as much as I could about that group and abbreviate it into a smaller crew with as little compromise as possible.

The books I purchased were on directing, sound recording, set design, cinematography, editing, and musical scoring. It was clear that I needed to be adequately familiar with all aspects of production before starting. I read and attempted to learn from several books I purchased on the subject of film directors. The books were enlightening, but in many respects were either anecdotal or delved deeply into the philosophies of the filmmakers. You would have had a need to know these detailed bits of information to appreciate the narrative. I was seeking meat and potatoes information, not esoteric, conceptual ideals. The books on basic directing were of greater overall value to me. They were to the point, without the artiness. I thought hard about what director's movies would be closest to mine and I came up with a cross between Woody Allen and the Farrelly brothers.

Two years later, and two weeks before my finished film was to debut, the Farrelly's, *There's Something About Mary* was released nationally. I went to see it on opening day and was totally startled to count eleven common thread gags in both movies. Was my writing and sense of humor that similar to the Farrellys? Interestingly, Bobby and Peter Farrelly grew up about thirty miles from me. From what I'd seen and read about them, I knew we shared a similar sense of humor. To experience it in that way was almost surrealistic. Maybe it's some kind of Rhode Island, geographic thing.

But I'm getting ahead of myself, so back to the books on directors. There was a lot written about the psychological interactions between the director and his cast. These areas were of particular interest to me. Being a sales rep I've always been aware of the psychology of relating to people. No relation means no common understanding.

A director's interaction with his cast is an extremely important dynamic that cannot be understated. I cannot imagine succeeding without it. A director's successful interaction with his cast only increases the chances that you'll both come out winners.

The books on cinematography were equally helpful in that they educated me in establishing the proper camera angles to appropriately convey what is going on in the scene. In addition to the camera angles, I learned the value of using the appropriate establishing shots for the scene to be shot. The master shot is wide, establishing the locations. The medium and close up shots are used to properly capture and accentuate what is being said in a scene. The most important dialogue necessitates the tightest composition. These are things that we as movie viewers are probably subliminally aware of, but it was good to read it and know for sure. The cinematography books also went into how to light a scene, and thankfully, my twenty-five years of experience as a part-time photographer allowed me to shortcut those chapters. My scan through those pages confirmed that I already knew this stuff. Although I appreciated the individual styles of cinematographers, I needed to use an approach that would be easy to maintain throughout this lengthy shoot.

I adopted a straight-forward style, using primarily flat lighting for all my interior scenes. My rationale was that most offices are lit with fluorescent, which are flat to begin with. I chose my lighting equipment sources to be compatible with the flat fluorescent, which I needed. Flat lighting would allow me to set up my lights and then move my subjects around as need be, without having to move the lights again.

This would be a major time saver when changing camera angles. Decisions like this one allowed me to film a lot more per day than if I had to move lights to create consistent light patterns viewed from different angles.

I would later regret that I didn't absorb the nuances of sound recording that were spelled out in the sound recording books. The book went into miking techniques in various situations, recording levels, and potential problems. The potential problem section was the one I'd wished I paid more attention to. You will read in Chapter 11 what I'm talking about. The scene I'm referring to was shot in a diner. My thirteen year old nephew, the sound recorder, and I, the default, resident expert, failed to notice the low drone of the central air conditioning system, which layered in with the dialogue spoken in the diner. The microphone was set up over the table between the speaking actors, just below the cursed air conditioning duct that was contaminating my recording. When we got to the post sound work at the end of the shooting, my sound editors told me that it would cost hundreds of dollars of corrections to improve, but not eliminate the drone. I agreed to pay for the attempted fix. It was improved, but you will notice upon reviewing that there is an unnatural ambient sound that "pulls you out of the scene" as the industry terms this affliction. A costly lesson attributed to on the job training.

The book I purchased on set design was one that I only scanned, primarily for basic familiarity. I made the decision not to get too involved, recognizing that without a budget and a dedicated set designer, it would be impossible to address this area properly. Being concerned with color schemes and décor of locations to complement what is happening or being said was way too much to contemplate when you know you'll be understaffed. However, it was good to know the basic rules of design so that I would avoid a blatant faux pas that would draw attention to my inexperience. I would have to rate the books I read on editing as extremely helpful in my shooting. There were countless examples and explanations of how scenes could or should be filmed, so that when they are assembled chronologically later, the visual flow would be smooth and as seamless as possible. That's as far as I read on the subject because I knew I would read the remaining detailed part of actual editing when the time came at the end of the shooting. No point in studying something I won't use for almost a year away. I'd only forget what I read by then and I didn't want to clutter my mind with any more info that I was already absorbing.

I did get one book on musical scoring but the subject was so far down on my need to know list that I gave it a scan and lumped it in with the editing book's back burner status. I assumed that I would be doing the editing myself via VCRs as Robert Rodriguez did. The musical score would totally be at the mercy of whoever would help me. I love music, but its writing is a total mystery to me. I have a tough time playing a kazoo in tune, just so you know where I'm coming from. As you can see, I was boning up and prepping to the max on actual production related subjects, yet I was taking a real leap of faith and a deferred attitude on post-production related matters. It was partially irresponsible in a way, but I also couldn't worry about everything or I would never get started.

Eventually, I amassed a library of books. By the time I found myself reading redundant information, I knew I was ready.

3

Help In Casting

Where to start? A sense of being overwhelmed set in as I attempted to prioritize pre-production. As confident as you need to be to undertake a first film, there's still that underlying doubt that's ever present. The inner voice that asks, "Can I really do this?" or "Am I biting off more than I can chew?"

I determined that the easiest task at hand would be the identification of locations for the shoot. I reasoned that getting through that part would ease me into the most major stage of all, casting. Baby stepping my way into this cave of uncertainty was to be my approach. "A journey of a thousand miles starts with the first step" and all those metaphors from years of watching "Kung Fu" on TV all came back to me. I went through the entire script and notated the locations required (answer: 60). I amusingly observed that if I wrote the script knowing that I'd be shooting it myself, I would have had the entire story take place in my living room. I would also have written the story with a total cast of two, maybe three people. The headcount for *BOXedMAN* is 43. Another big number. I'll worry about casting after I deal with location hunting.

Having written my script before deciding to actually shoot it was a problem. I wrote it to be a funny script, without any regard to production considerations. Now I was gonna pay. I had to find every single location. A movie theater, several restaurants, diners, a nursing home, outdoor shopping centers, a barber shop, exteriors both night and day, just to name a sampling. You get the picture. I was in way over my head. Fortunately, my day job gave me a huge leg up on scouting office locations. When I'd see a location that met with my pre-visualized needs, I'd ask the customer or prospect if I could film there. I would explain that I couldn't pay them rent, but would acknowledge them in the credits of the film. It was amazing to find that no one turned me down. People I don't even know didn't turn me down. It reaffirmed my faith in people. Most will do good given the chance.

When I spoke to filmmakers from New York and Los Angeles I got a different story. They have to pay for all locations along with permits and insurance to cover any possible eventualities. This is enough proof to encourage independent filmmakers to shoot in smaller cities. Smaller cities don't view filmmaking as an interruption that warrants compensation. I wouldn't have been able to afford to shoot 60 locations if I had to pay for them.

I went through the entire script and started listing locations both interior and exterior. Now I really had a handle on what was ahead. One hundred and forty scenes spread over sixty locations. I told myself I couldn't dwell on the enormity of the project because I might have come to my senses and bailed out before I began. I used the analogy of climbing a mountain. If you look at the whole thing, you wouldn't want to climb it. Dealing with it ten feet at a time isn't as mind crippling and hopefully before you know it, you're half way up. That's what I kept telling myself.

All my spare time was consumed with location scouting and reading books to prepare for the shoot. My large laserdisc movie collection was another source of researchable help in planning my scenes out. Many times, I'd read a scene in my script and remember a film I'd seen with a scene that might resemble it. Even a remote resemblance could lead to resolving a "how-to" question. This practice allowed me to storyboard in my mind and resolve questions of execution.

Years later, I read that Jim Cameron used the same practice when shooting *Titanic*. He was indecisive on how to open the film. His answer came after viewing the opening scenes of approximately seventy laserdiscs accompanied by a bottle of tequila. I'm not sure how much influence the tequila had, but referencing other people's work is clearly a creative catalyst.

Director's commentary tracks on laserdiscs were another big aid in planning. A party scene in my film had to have spoken dialogue in the midst of a party with music and ambient crowd noise simultaneously. (See Chapter 5, Sunday Sept 21.) How do I do this? Well, the answer is on the Mrs. Doubtfire collector's laser disc set. Chris Columbus, the director, explains that in a scene involving a children's party, he faced the same dilemma. His solution, which became mine, is that the background people in the scene move their lips silently as if they're talking. You just add the ambient background music and background dialogue in post-production. So when you're filming the scene, you only have the speaking actor's dialogue to record. Very cool tricks of the trade. By the time January '97 came around, I was feeling very prepared.

Coinciding with my preparatory planning was

the local excitement generated by Stephen Spielberg's setting up shop in Newport for his film *Amistad.* Spielberg was turning Washington Square back 150 years. All signs of the present day...lamp poles, telephone wires, parking meters and sidewalks...received cosmetic treatment or temporary removal. The streets were filled with dirt to the heights of the sidewalks disguising the curbs. An entire building, "the jail house," was erected in St. Anne's Square. The stone-faced building was made of fiberglass panels over a wood framed shell so realistically that it looked real even up close. Their shooting schedule was approximately one month in duration, shooting from early morning until mid-evening. I intended to try to watch shooting both before I went to work in the morning and after work at night. I even went so far as to submit photos of myself at a casting call in hopes of getting first-hand experience.

Although I didn't get cast, I did get to shake Stephen Spielberg's hand on the first week of production. I was hoping that something spiritual might pass through the handshake and give me good luck. Watching Spielberg work was both inspirational and a diversion from my personal pressing schedule. I had to get going on equipment buying.

I called several used camera stores listed in

American Cinematographer Magazine. I narrowed down the choice of cameras to three after comparing prices and features. The cameras I considered were all built in the mid to late 60's, back in the days before video replaced film as the evening news medium. The evolution to video orphaned thousands of 16mm movie cameras. They're all available now for prices ranging from $4000 to $8000. A lot of money for a thirty year old camera but a lot less than a present day $100,000 new 16mm camera. The new cameras have time codes and many bells and whistles that an old camera lacks, but when you're a know nothing neophyte, you can't miss something you don't know exists. The only considerations I had were handhold ability and crystal sync motor. The crystal sync motor keeps the camera shooting at 24 frames per second without variation; an important feature as professional DAT recorders (sound), and eventually digital recorders, also have quartz crystal timing devices in them that keeps them recording at non-varying timing. If either your camera or sound recorders were to vary the slightest amount, you'd be faced with people's voices not aligning with their lip movement.

Robert Rodriquez explained that that's what he dealt with while shooting his $7000 *El Mariachi*. Robert used a non-sync camera (imperfect timing) and a Radio Shack portable cassette recorder (imperfect timing). With two imperfect devices in hand, you are, in effect, creating infinite variables of deviation. He had to sync his footage one line at a time using visual means rather than the accepted method of using a slate.

A scene is slated not only for identification, but for lining up the motion picture image with the sound recorder. The editor in post-production indexes the frame where the upper slate makes contact with the lower slate. He then indexes the sound recorder to where the sound of the 'bang' is heard. He then runs the film and sound together throughout the entire scene to sync them together. So much easier than Robert's method. Robert did it his way because that's the only equipment he had at his disposal for his no budget film. Seeing as I wasn't trying to break the record he established for a feature film under $7000, I decided to spend more money up front for a crystal sync camera and a DAT recorder. Recognizing that I was about to bite off way more than I could chew, I felt I would rather run up a little more debt and keep my aggravation quotient down. My hair was and is grey enough, I didn't want it to turn shock white.

After discussing my project with several camera shops on both coasts, I decided to do business with Du-All camera in New York City. George Gal and his sons Steve and Jeff run the shop. George Gal turned out to be a renowned camera repairman who had authored books on 16mm cameras and their operation. He is one of three people in the world who services the ECLAIR line of cameras, a now out-of-business French camera manufacturer. He offers in-house service and, bearing in mind I was acquiring a 30-year-old camera, it was an important consideration. The deal clincher was Du-All's one-year warrantee. This is not a typo, ONE YEAR. All other stores offered 30-90 days. This definitely brought peace of mind considering that a production schedule like mine would be approximately six months in length.

Keeping the surprise factor to a minimum was always underlining all my decisions. Having never handled a motion picture camera before, I felt it important to line up my visit to Du-All for a day when all three cameras were in stock for my consideration. I kept contact with George weekly, surveying his ever-changing used inventory. In late March '97, I called and he had just taken in a trade completing a full house. All three different cameras under one roof! I asked him to hold off selling any of them till I came in to see them the next day.

What I thought would be an hour visit turned into a four hour shopping trip. It took an hour to get the feel of the Éclair, the Cinema Products

CP16, and the Arriflex 16 BL, as well as learning how differently the film loaded between brands. Talk about give and take considerations. The camera that loaded the easiest felt the worst when your shoulder mounted it. The camera that shoulder mounted the most comfortably had the highest price. It took another three hours to weigh all considerations and finally decide on the Arriflex 16 BL. It was the most expensive of the three but a decision I never regretted. As I proudly cashed out with a $6500 purchase, a young man and his girlfriend came in with a check for $25,000 for a newer than mine, used Arriflex camera. I'm not a filmmaker for two minutes and I'm already feeling peer pressure envy. Life's unfair. Something always seems to happen to dampen your spirits just when you're feeling good. Leaving the store in Manhattan, I quickly forgot my envy, as I walked down 42nd St. proudly carrying my new camera in its case.

The entire next day, my mind raced with questions regarding the use of my camera. Juggling these thoughts with the everyday tasks and demands of my sales job was enough to occupy my conscious and sub-conscious mind. Enough so that when I stopped by my office at the end of the day, I hadn't noticed the light on my phone, indicating a recorded voice mail message. Voice mail was just installed and I was unfamiliar with its use. I finally retrieved the message several days later, when I became aware that there was a message. The message was from the AMISTAD casting office. The message was: Please call tonight for further instructions. You have been cast in tomorrow's shoot (this was now two days after the message was left). I quickly called the casting office, but of course it was too late. The scene had already been shot and they were now on the last day of shooting. If I had it in me to cause self-inflicted injury, I'd be dead now. That oversight caused me to beat myself up mentally for an entire month.

With the camera purchase now behind me, it was time to concentrate on the sound recorder (DAT). I checked mail order houses for pricing and determined that the portable SONY TCD D10 PRO II was the model to buy, but the price was in the $4000 range. My calls to L.A. used dealers found prices in the $2500 range, which was still more than I wanted to spend. A few weeks later, success! A music shop in New London, CT, had an ad in a local music industry paper that led me to call, finding they had a used Sony DAT recorder for $1300.

I couldn't drive there fast enough to purchase it. This is the kind of purchase that was perfect timing. As I write this, I still can't believe I found that deal, just when I needed it. One more piece of equipment down, and several more to go.

The next months of prep was spent on the phone with several mail order photo supply shops in N.Y. investigating and purchasing light stands, tripods, lights, scrims, reflectors, etc. Every night after work, questions and answers and decisions had to be made, not to mention money spent. As April went quickly by, the hanging question about casting was most definitely on my mind. I have a cast of 43 actors to assemble and I've got to learn where to find them, how to audition them, how to weed them out, and then rehearse and direct them.

I reference my laser disc of *Brothers McMullen*. The writer, director, and actor Edward Burns has a commentary track on which he explains how he put his cast together. He took out an ad in a Long Island newspaper advertising his need for non-paid actors. He surprisingly received 1500 replies. That alone gave me a comforting feeling. The thing that concerned me the most about that approach is getting people responding that couldn't act and maybe have never performed before. I certainly didn't have the time to weed through a large number of respondents, so in April, I contacted the largest performing arts group in Providence, RI. Trinity Repertory Theater, which had a renowned apprenticeship program. Unfortunately, I learned that they are Equity or SAG members, which meant that they could only work for pay. I explained my predicament and was told that there are provisions and exceptions, but you have to put up a $1000 bond and some contractual considerations. The money and the paperwork was another hurdle that I didn't need. Abandoning that approach led me to plan B. Plan B was contacting a number of dinner theater playhouses in Rhode Island.

One of these was in my town, The Newport Playhouse and Cabaret Restaurant. It was run by Jonathan Perry and his uncle, Matt Siravo. I had watched a few of their well-performed, entertaining comedies and identified some actors I could easily and gladly use.

But a visit to City Nights Dinner Theater in Pawtucket, RI, was the most pivotal event that would ultimately affect the quality of my cast.

The theater director Ernie Medeiros was sympathetic to my pitch. I explained to Ernie that I was a neophyte that needed some pointers in casting. He invited me and anyone from my crew to attend a two-day audition for an upcoming play. It would be my first exposure to the backstage of any performing arts productions.

Not only would I learn how an audition is conducted but I could also scope out his prospects for my own productions. This is too good! I thought. I gathered up several of my crew members to attend the audition with me. Watching the process not only taught me how to conduct my own, but allowed me the opportunity to find several actors for my film. I approached them individually during lulls in the action, told them of my movie, and got a phone number. After two consecutive nights of auditions, I felt pretty comfortable with my observations. I actually developed a feel for the process and am pleased and surprised that I formed opinions about the auditions. I have identified approximately 10 actors that I can use for my audition. 43 roles is what I have to fill. I was still way short. I told Ernie this as I started to fret. He extended an offer for me to come in another time and peruse his extensive file of headshots amassed over a decade. Another blessing!

Days later, I returned to spend over four hours pulling close to two hundred headshots from a plastic filing bin. This was a virtual treasure trove of head shots leading to potential possibilities and answered prayers. Ernie spent time going over the photos, telling me the experience and talent level of my choices. He created a huge shortcut for me. We collectively narrowed the list down to approximately one hundred actors. I took down their names and phone numbers, thanking Ernie for simplifying my life.

Now that I had casting partially under control,

I thought it time to turn to the ugliest aspect of independent filmmaking—MONEY. One thing I knew for sure is that I didn't have enough of it. And I didn't want to take out a home equity loan. Coppola did it for *Apocalypse Now,* but I'm not him and I'm not making *Apocalypse Now.* As I mentioned, hunting down investors to back a filmmaker with zero experience was too unsavory a task. I could just imagine the strange looks I'd have gotten and just knew it wasn't an option. Facing a bank loan officer with a similar pitch was equally unsettling. So, I resigned myself to the most popular form of financing known to filmmakers, the credit card. I applied for a pile of them all offering low introductory rates. The two biggest expenses I would face regularly would be film and processing, so I opened accounts with Eastman Kodak and Du-Art Labs. In my talks with Du-Art, the question came up as to how I would edit my film. I told them I was planning on using two VCR's and a used JVC video editor I had recently purchased for this purpose. That's how Robert Rodriguez did *El Mariachi,* I told them. Silence at the other end. Then a pearl of wisdom.

"It's very difficult that way," said my guiding voice on the phone.

I explained that I was highly motivated to get my film made and would deal with the difficulty.

They advised that when they processed the film, I should order the videocassettes with time codes and key codes burned on the copies, just in the event I might come to my senses and have the film edited on an Avid digital system.

I confessed that I didn't have the money for a professional edit, but would consider their advice. "I'll let you know when I send in my first rolls of film for processing."

After hanging up, I remembered that the film critic of the Providence Journal Michael Janousonis interviewed a Rhode Islander two years before who had received two Academy Awards and two Emmy Awards for co-founding Avid Corp. and their groundbreaking digital editing system. I had saved the article for future reference (God knows why). The time of reference was now. I called information to track Tom Ohanian down in hopes he could give me advice on this seemingly troublesome aspect of film production.

I got Tom on the telephone and was pleasantly surprised by his accessibility. I anticipated less. Our first call lasted for 45 minutes spanning movies we enjoyed—our tastes, likes, and dislikes. Tom realized how determined I was to make my film. He asked if I could send the script to him. I told him I would and he said he would call me after reading it.

Several weeks later he called to tell me he had read it on a red eye flight from L.A and couldn't stop laughing. He woke many fellow passengers as he laughed out loud. Tom told me that if I shot it like I wrote it, I would have a funny picture and he wanted to be a part of it. He wanted to edit my picture, he informed me, and that I would have a miserable experience trying to do it myself with VCRs. Attempting to synchronize the moving lips on the screen of the VCR with the recorded dialogue on DAT tape would be insanely time consuming. I reiterated that I was on an anemic budget and couldn't possibly afford it. He insisted on doing it and told me, "I'll give you a price you won't refuse."

A week later, he sent me a quote I couldn't refuse. To this day, and throughout my life, I'll be indebted to Tom Ohanian for saving my sanity. Loose ends were coming together and getting tied up. I was starting to feel a sense of control.

Next came crew, the people behind the camera. I polled friends, relatives, and anyone that might have time on their hands in the coming half year or so. Asking someone to commit a half of a year or more of their precious personal time is enough to give anyone second thoughts. That was my best, inexperienced guesstimate at the amount of time required to shoot the film on a part-time basis. The positive respondents committed to, "Sure, as I have a free day, etc."

Several friends and cousins filled in here and there. My 13-year-old nephew, David Mack, handled sound almost every day. My good friend, Guy Weston, handled camera operator duties most of the production, and my girlfriend, Carol Kent, handled script supervisor, focus puller, and miscellaneous positions for the entire production. This was a surprise because before we started, she made the statement, "Don't count on me every day because I need some time to myself." Once we got started though, she got into it and chose to work every day, thus proving that filmmaking, regardless of the difficulties of the project, beats working a regular job anytime. A true labor of love. That was the unanimous conclusion of ALL who worked on *BOXedMAN*.

Coinciding with all these concerns was my first shoot the following weekend. My film was to open with a college graduation sequence. This was a one-chance-only, no opportunity to re-shoot till next year event. I was becoming enveloped in pressure situations. I'd scoped out all the college campuses in the general Providence area and had determined that URI's layout would be the easiest to shoot and give me the greatest ease of filming.

Saturday, May 18

Early that morning, my cousin Laura Pasyanos was graduating with honors from Salve Regina University in Newport at an outdoor service. I shot some footage there as I was attending the ceremony, but chose not to do greater coverage because it was held under a tent, which didn't coincide with the opening scene I'd envisioned.

After the ceremony, I packed up and traveled to URI with my nephew and assistant Dave, to film parts of their ceremony that I would edit together to represent one graduation. The filming went uneventfully, thanks to my advanced planning. What was unplanned was my prior carelessness. I was told to run a test roll through the camera when I purchased it, but felt it wasn't necessary. What could go wrong? Well, I'll tell you.

I shot the scenes, processed the film, and found that there was a light leak in the camera. The leaks caused a flash of white light to disrupt every approximately 15 seconds of footage. Due to the disruption of the white flash, the title, director, producer etc. credits were slugged in at those points. This unfortunate problem determined and forced the opening credits to be created and cut the way they are now. Not what I had in mind, but I had to live with it. I did say that this was a one-shot opportunity and Murphy's Law strikes at every chance it gets.

The camera was sent back to Du-All in N.Y. where the problem was fixed. I got the camera back and ran a test roll which was OK. Now, I was really ready. The next shoot wouldn't happen till I cast my film. I hoped I would find my cast soon. The time had now come for me to set up my own auditions.

I called around and found a nearby banquet hall that I could rent to run my auditions. I then called all my potential prospects to invite them to the audition. At this time, I explained that this was a non-paying endeavor. I told them that they would get paid down the road if I'm successful in getting the film sold. No one said no. Everyone was in. I smiled at the realization that we were all in the same boat. I was ready to give up over a year of my life and go into hock for God knows how much, and for how long, for a shot at Hollywood. We all want it.

I scheduled the auditions on the ninth and twenty-third of June. I chose two dates, two weeks apart, to allow for their convenience. A note on convenience. The state of Rhode Island may be the smallest state, but its populace has an aversion to traveling, especially if it involves bridges. It is the Ocean State and there are several bridges that connect the state together. It is a psychological barrier that is both metaphoric and factual. The hall was in Pawtucket, close enough to most of my locations, so that I wouldn't have to worry about people showing up.

The ninth of June came fast and I rounded up a panel to observe the auditions and two friends to videotape the actors as they read selected lines. Once the actors had assembled in the hall, I would give them copies of the dialogue spoken by the character in the script they reminded me of most visually. The readings were going very well till we got to the dialogue for the lead characters. Was I shocked to find that the dialogue I asked them to read was wooden when delivered out loud! The scene they were reading was an important scene, so I cringed with each reading of what clearly was awkward dialogue in need of a rewrite. The dialogue was stilted and amateurishly unnatural. What was I thinking writing it? How did I not see this before having prospective actors reading it? I did my best to hide my embarrassment, tune out the dialogue, and concentrate on their performance. I hoped that all the other actors would not pass judgment and consider leaving the audition. Fortunately for me, no one left. In the end, I feel I was objective and, over the two nights, I had made countless decisions that were good. There were also some other surprises, i.e. read an actor for one role and found that they were better suited for another. Viewing the videotapes in the quiet of my home helped tremendously in seeing possibilities that weren't apparent in the busy atmosphere of the audition. All in all, I was making progress, moving ever closer to a start date.

My next step was to contact the chosen actors to see if they were interested, and send them all the pages of the script that pertained to their character. I had already broken down the script into groupings of locations, characters, groups of characters, and time of day so that I could lump together pairings for the production schedule. I hadn't read any books on the subject of planning, so I did what I thought was logical. Breaking down the script by characters, locations, specific days, and groupings of actors made sense. I would then evaluate the shooting possibilities every scheduled day. For instance, if I was shooting at a particular office building on Saturday morning, I would get all the actors there regardless of where in the story they were. I also broke down the script into hypothetical story days, i.e. absolute different days, relative to the whole story. In that way, actors were told we're shooting scenes #7, 56, and 103 and these were on days 2, 15, and 21 in the story. The actors were made responsible for keeping track of what they wore for day 2, 15, and 21. For some it wasn't a problem. The protagonist, who is in just about every scene, would have it the hardest. He would have 30+ story days of clothing to keep track of. Surprisingly, out of the whole production there is only one goof up on clothing and no one has detected it except me. Hey, when you can't afford a wardrobe department, you do what you got to do. I felt leaving the hairstyles and clothing record keeping up to the actors wasn't really asking too much. I did need all the help I could get. The administrative production planning I had to do was going to consume all weekday evenings. Shooting was going to be every weekend till finished. Throughout both screen tests, discoveries were made. The surprises came when my pre-conceived expectations were proved wrong and another match was made with a minor change in perspective.

One of the treasures of my search was finding Terri Leander who I would cast as the protagonist's love interest. Terri had it all, looks, acting skills, and smarts. I concluded after all the screen tests that she was the right choice for the vulnerable character Bonnie. She was right except for one problem. In real life, Terri was now four months pregnant. Not showing yet, but would be soon. I deduced that I'd be okay as long as I shot all her scenes first.

Second problem. All her scenes were with her protagonist love interest. That role was still not cast. Boy, did I have a problem. I auditioned a score of young actors who were the right age but not one of them was the Rick Williams character that existed in my mind and was in almost every scene in the movie.

I talked with Ernie at City Nights Theater about my dilemma. I was starting to question my judgment. Was I being too picky? Ernie was a big fan of Terri's, so he commended me on my taste. He suggested I look at an actor that was gaining a following at Trinity Rep in Providence. Eric Tucker worked with Ernie in his earlier career before making it to Trinity Rep. I called Eric and he was very interest in reading for me. Eric turned out to be a stand out performer as expected. He had talent, range, and enthusiasm for the role. After auditioning him several times, I concluded he wasn't right for the part. Eric was tall and had a self-assured look. Rick Williams was an underdog, possibly short, straight man, that had everything happen to him. I felt badly enough about not choosing him that I called to explain my decision. He was a real pro who understood. I periodically read articles about him in the paper, telling of his performances all over the country, and I feel good knowing he's doing well.

The only thing I didn't enjoy about casting is rejecting people that were clearly talented, but not right for the part. Being a salesman makes me in-nately sensitive. Rejection is part and parcel of selling. You get more rejections than acceptances, so a thick skin is a required personality trait. It does not make you immune to feeling bad though. I know how I feel when I'm turned down, so I feel bad when I have to do it to others. All my casting decisions were based on matching the actor to the characters I had written. This could only serve to get me closer to the ideal. Remember, this was my first movie so typecasting was a shortcut. Type-casting was also my way of addressing a fear that was planted months before.

A friend put me in touch with his cousin in New Jersey who had made an independent feature a few years ago.

"Call him, he could give you some tips," was my friend's suggestion.

I called and got a tip that chilled me. The film that my friend's cousin made had a fatal flaw, attributed to the miscasting of the lead role. A flaw that didn't become apparent until it was too late. His picture was a total disaster because the lead actor was not believable. He said the movie was unwatchable. The big tip was, "Be careful in casting." Those words kept me on edge throughout casting. His picture was disastrously ruined.

So there I was, looking for the male lead to play opposite my pregnant female lead. Scary scenario. I made calls to every theater director in the state of RI describing my ideal protagonist. I explained that if I didn't find my lead soon, I'd lose my leading lady for at least nine months unless I recast the role again, which felt like a circuitous route to nowhere.

Salvation came days later. One theater director called another theater director and they called me with a referral…a stand-up comic named, Richard "Ace" Aceto. His description sure seemed like a match. I called Ace and he sounded excited to get a call about a motion picture opportunity. We met a few days later and he sure looked like what I was looking for. I told him my female lead choice was Terri Leander and he smiled knowingly. He and Terri had starred opposite each other in *A Midsummer's Night's Dream* at the Barker Theater in Providence six months earlier. He thought I'd made a great choice. But, remember, I'd been forewarned…miscast and you're dead. I told Ace I'd like to do a reading with Terri that I could shoot on video to see how they looked together. Ace was working two jobs and time was a premium.

We agreed to meet at a grassy median strip of an upscale neighborhood in Providence, RI. The area was a short walking distance for Terri. It was a slightly busy area, and a tad livelier than the cemetery Terri and I had ultimately used the week before. The male actor that Terri had read opposite requested a quieter location than the noisy rendezvous location. The nearest quiet spot we could think of was the Swan Point Cemetery, so we did. Kind of weird, but at that point, what is conventional?

When Ace arrived at the location, I noticed his license plate had his initials and the numbers 68.

"Is that the year you were born?" I asked.

"Sure is," came his quick reply.

"That makes you 29?"

"Yup."

"Your name is Rick, and you're 29?"

"Right again."

I tell him my script is the story of a 29-year-old guy named Rick who takes his first serious job as a salesman. He then informs me that he just got hired by a pharmaceutical company, as a salesman, in real life. Have I mentioned omen?

At this point, the hairs on the back of my neck were standing up. But I'd a screen test to shoot and I didn't want superstition to come into play. I shot for approximately 10-15 minutes as they read the scenes that they're both in. I was very happy with how they looked together.

I told Rick, "You've got it if you want it, but you have to read the script first. I've got to know you're really committed."

I couldn't afford for him to change his mind mid-picture and leave me with a pile of bills and useless celluloid. Not that anyone in their right mind would do such a thing. These are just some of the insecurities and crazy thoughts that come to you when you're jumping off a cliff.

Ace took the script and called me two days later. He loved it and wanted to do it. Only one problem, and there is always one, he'd started his new sales job and had to go away for a month of schooling in North Carolina. We had one week before he went and I knew I had to shoot all of Terri's full body shots that coming weekend.

I called Kodak and placed my first film order which would be shipped Fed-Ex overnight. One box = five rolls = fifty-five minutes of filming = $650.00. Whew! I'd now officially entered the deep end of the pool. The time had come to consult my shot group schedule. The schedule grouped shots by a) actors, b) locations, c) combinations of actors, d) combinations of actors and locations, and e) day and night. I had references, cross references, and cross references to the cross references. This was accomplished, as I mentioned before, by writing up spreadsheets of categories and then combing the script for all categories listed. A very tedious and time consuming process. An absolute necessity if you want to shoot as efficiently as possible. This is key as you travel down the long road of production. I assume large productions do it the same way because the alternative would be maddening.

I added one more sub category. Ace and Terri full body shots. My first weekend of shooting would start on a late Friday afternoon of the upcoming week. It was the eleventh of July. The scene was Rick and Bonnie having a picnic by a lighthouse illuminated by a setting sun. My hopes were to not only shoot the scene, but to include the setting sun at the tail end of the scene, time permitting. There was also a scene later in the picture where the Rick and Bonnie characters meet at the same location on another day. Rick went there to spread his grandmother's ashes in the water. With luck and a bit of hustle, I hoped to shoot that scene also before darkness. It was extremely optimistic planning, even from an optimist's point of view. The actors planned to bring a change of clothes just in case.

4

First Day Of Shooting

Friday, July 11

We all met at my house after work on that Friday and caravan over to Castle Hill in Newport. We quickly set up and weeks of anxiety and anticipation were brought to an end. Ace and Terri rehearsed their lines as I reviewed procedures with my friend Guy Weston, camera operator, and David Mack, my 13-year-old nephew on sound. The crew was rounded out by my girlfriend Carol Kent as script supervisor, my niece Liz Mack, and my cousins Duke and Steve Pasyanos as production assistants. At this early stage, I didn't know how much assistance would be necessary. I basically invited anyone with a curiosity and time on their hands to show up. It only took one cycle of calling "rolling," "action," and then "cut" to feel at home.

For twenty-five years, I'd been a part-time wedding photographer where, for the better part of an eight-hour day, I'd arrange, light, and compose people for lasting images that people would enjoy for years. Well, this wasn't very much different. The major difference was now my subjects were moving and speaking.

I cannot describe how at ease I felt in this capacity. I knew this was where I belonged and what I wanted to do for the rest of my life. I had taken the dialogue for this scene and determined that shooting this in master shot was adequate. A master shot is also referred to as the establishing shot. It's usually wide-angled in nature, which shows the locale and the relative position of the actors in the overall scene. Balancing economic (film=$) considerations and effective storytelling is a serious consideration. Limitless budgets would allow you to shoot coverage from different camera angles and varying degrees of close up to allow the editor freedom to experiment and find the best way to tell the story. I didn't have the financial luxury.

I also rationalized that Woody Allen, throughout his prolific career of shooting a movie a year over the past 50 years, uses this method exclusively as an expedient and efficient technique to get a film "in the can."

I did cut to close-ups for a portion of the dialogue to accent the scene's impact and to break up the master shot. This netted me a scene with more impact without adding significantly to the amount of film used. Just as soon as I completed filming the dialogue scene, I changed the camera angle composing for the establishing sunset shot with the picnicking couple in the foreground.

Ten seconds of film later, Ace and Terri hustled to their cars to change up for the scene where Rick scatters his grandmother's cremated remains into the sea. The scene was originally an unoriginal graveside scene with casket and mourners. The scene would have required a priest, mourners dressed in black, etc. Seen it a hundred times. I'm friends with a funeral director in town and I planned to ask if I could borrow a casket and other essentials for the scene. Thankfully, the cremated ashes concept came to me in pre-production, which simplified everything both financially and logistically, and, interestingly, in both in film and real life. I'd asked my funeral director friend what was the best substitute for cremated remains and he answered...beach sand, like you find on Newport Beach near our homes.

So I filled a velvet drawstring bag with sand to use in the scene. Ace and Terri rushed back to find us prepped to shoot the scene in the now disappearing daylight. Because the scene would be layered with music it was shot M.O.S (mit out sound). The term came about when German directors, working in early Hollywood, would pronounce mit for the word WITH. "Without sound" came out of their mouths as "mit out sound;" hence, a new acronym was born.

During filming, Ace walked to the water's edge solemnly and slowly poured the sand out of the bag into the water. I had filled the bag completely, which made the scene run endlessly.

My cousin, knowing we were filming MOS, yelled out, "Grandma must have been a big lady!"

Well, Ace had all he could do not to burst out laughing while trying to remain solemn. As soon as I called "cut," we all laughed, then turned serious again, rotating the camera 180 degrees toward land and quickly setting up the scene where Terri approached Ace after the ashes scene.

The light was almost non-existent at this point and I only had time for one take as I did with the previous scene. My first day of shooting and I was already familiar with a quick paced, shotgun style of shooting. The scene was set up and shot so quickly that I got a corner of my camera case in the shot as I started filming but decided to continue only because I knew we couldn't do another take before final darkness fell. It was that close.

The Coen Brothers have a similar gaff in their first picture, *Blood Simple,* that apparently hadn't hurt them or their director of photography, I reasoned. Hopefully, this can be addressed if I get distribution. As soon as I called "cut" on the scene, we embraced, shook hands, and congratulated each other for surviving the first of what will become a totally unknown number of days of shooting. We packed up in the darkness and set up the rendezvous of the next morning's shoot.

Saturday, July 12

This would be our first day of multi-location shooting. The early morning session was planned to avoid real shoppers in the outdoor mall locale that we were filming in. Not having a permit or extra people for crowd control made this the only choice. I hoped that my finished product wouldn't raise the questions, a) why aren't there any other shoppers? And, b) why is this Bonnie character pregnant? Damn insecurities!

The scene of Bonnie and Rick shopping before going on their picnic went very well. This also included the reaction shot where Rick looked at a girl getting out of a car that physically wasn't there. I would shoot and cut that in whenever I'd find the person to play the character described as "woman with great legs getting out of her car."

We completed the close-up reaction shots and called it a wrap for that location well before the stores opened. I now know that this film will be finished. All through pre-production there's always that touch of doubt that you dare not mention or you might give it life or legitimacy. I now felt I was going to be okay.

We packed up and prepared to head north to our next locations. When I say we, I mean we. The actors became part of the crew in moving equipment. No egos on this production, I can assure you. We would be shooting scenes where Rick meets Bonnie in the office. This scene would include the reaction shot as they attract each other, with the subsequent small talk that followed. From there, there would be a clothing change and we would shoot the scene where Rick asks Bonnie out on a date. The scenes were shot at my personal studio, Crystal Thermoplastics in Cumberland, Rhode Island. The Brown family that owns Crystal Thermoplastics are friends of mine who were extremely generous in not only allowing me to shoot in their building but gave me the keys and alarm codes to come and go as my production schedule required. The fact that their building has numerous individual private offices afforded me the opportunity to use this locale to represent just as many different office locations. It was also an ideal fallback position to use when outdoor shooting couldn't be done due to inclement weather. Having this available was an incredible luxury. One of the many blessings that came my way.

It's the rock soup theory. The tale of a guy on the street, with a pot of water boiling, with only a rock inside. Passersby would inquire what he's up to and he'd reply, "I'm making soup."

They'd answer back, "You can't do that, you've only got a rock." "How about some carrots?" They'd give him carrots. Another would offer potatoes and on and on until eventually he had real soup.

The kindness and generosity of others toward those in need cannot be underestimated.

We finished shooting those two scenes and were on hold for three weeks. Ace was leaving for training on his new job in North Carolina. We went over the schedule that we'd be shooting as soon as he returned. I prayed that Terri's pregnancy wouldn't be showing by that time. There were still a few more scenes where her full body would be visible. We bade each other goodbye and wished Ace well on his three week training.

I was then officially shut down. There was nothing for me to shoot because Ace was in practically every scene in the movie.

With only a weekend of filmmaking experience to my credit, I'd gained some insight and experience with which to aid me in production planning. I spent the next three weeks in production planning while attempting to firm up loose ends that I could foresee over the next five months. I kept in touch with Ace, giving him the evolving production schedule so that he had adequate time to prep for his scenes when he returned. I tried not to be too demanding of him by expecting him to prep his lines while studying for his new, highly-technical line of work. Our collective understanding of the importance of getting all of Terri's scenes done before she started to show kept me from appearing heartless. It was understood that we'd be shooting as soon as he got off the plane.

5

Ace Is Back

Sunday, August 3

The three weeks flew by and Ace was back as planned for the August 3rd shoot. The first shot on the agenda was Rick walking up the hallway to Bonnie's office at the end of the movie. We also shot the scene where Rick enters Bonnie's office, where she flirts with him, and flashes him a leg shot.

Once completed, we left the Crystal Thermoplastics building and headed down the street to Davenport's Restaurant to shoot the scene of Ace driving into the parking spot and entering the restaurant for his date with Bonnie. During the editing process, it was decided that this scene was unnecessary, so it was left on the cutting room floor. We edited digitally, so technically speaking, there was no physical film to snip and drop onto the floor. The term is still used, but its new definition is that the file of the scene just remains dormant on a hard drive. Oh well, this wouldn't be the last item shot that when reviewed in the context of the whole was deemed not worth inclusion. These scenes were filmed pretty quickly, and we were now faced with the fact that we were shut down for another month as Ace had to return to North Carolina for another month of job training.

Sunday, September 7

I'd set up the day of shooting at the Davenport Restaurant in Cumberland, RI, where we had shot the scene of Ace pulling up to the restaurant the previous month.

Greg and his mother Claire Davenport were very accommodating in allowing me to come in early in the morning and shoot until they opened at 11 a.m.. The restaurant had two sections, a main dining room and a coffee shop style annex, which was perfect for me because I was shooting two different scenes intended to be two different locations, so we were able to get them both without leaving.

The first scene was Bonnie and Rick going for

coffee after the cremation ashes scattering scene. The scene was set up with Rick and Bonnie facing each other in a booth. While filming this coffee shop scene, my nephew Dave, who was holding the microphone boom over the actors, got a little careless and allowed the boom to drift down into the scene. Guy, the camera operator, saw it and tried to signal to me what was happening. He couldn't remove his eye from the viewfinder because by design, light would enter the eye piece and fog the film. This has to do with the reflex viewing system. So, here's Guy, trying to keep his head stationary against the viewfinder, while wildly raising his right hand to signal that the microphone is in the picture.

I saw this and tapped Dave to move the mike up. Meanwhile, the actors stayed in role, continuing what was the best take of this scene. During the editing process we had to zoom this scene to remove the microphone from the top of the frame. Here was a mistake that became an accidental improvement. This scene is an emotional scene which should have been staged as a tighter composition. My decision during pre-production was to shoot everything in master scenes (ala Woody Allen) because it's very efficient. There are times you need to make exceptions but I was so single minded that my objectivity was clouded. This accident that necessitated a zoom correction gave me the framing I should have had. Sometimes, luck does beat out skill.

The other scene we needed to film is where Rick and Bonnie meet after work for dinner, so we used the restaurant side of Davenports for that scene. They both changed up for the totally different day shoot. They sat in a circular booth and talked about their workday. This is where Rick learns that his general manager, Edward Cox, is sexually harassing Bonnie. The battle lines are now drawn, and this would be the end of what would be considered Act 2 of the classic 3 Act structure.

We were satisfied that we got both of those scenes in the can. Satisfied and relieved because Bonnie's real-life pregnancy was just starting to show and having both of those scenes with her seated with a table in front of her helped to disguise the real-world situation. We were now done with all of Bonnie's speaking scenes. A big sigh of relief from yours truly.

We successfully got all the shots we needed before the restaurant had to open. From there we drove to a daycare center where the parking lot resembled a mall parking lot. This scene was where Bonnie and Rick pull up to the Beavertail Point shopping district. It was now noon and all our planned shooting was completed. Because of collective planning, the next shoot wouldn't be until September Twenty-first.

Sunday, September 21

Next up, the garden cocktail party for the post-graduation scene. My neighbor Shirley Reiss graciously offered her yard, tables, and punchbowls for this scene. I called dozens of my friends to dress up, drink, eat finger food, and get some screen time playing the parents of students. I asked all of the college age friends to bring caps and gowns for authenticity. My neighbor Shirley was so happy to have referred her friend Ethel Groff to play the grandmother in my film. This became a problem because in one scene where Rick is speaking to his grandmother, Shirley looked at Ethel proudly throughout the entire take. A very peculiar occurrence in the context of the scene. I was so concentrating on the performance that I didn't notice this was happening. You can imagine my shock when I watched the dailies a week later and saw that Shirley had ruined all the takes with her hypnotic gaze toward Ethel. Another batch of wasted film. Conveniently, I was unhappy with the way the scene played out aside from Shirley's stare. The dialogue was so ponderous, it was a repeat of how I felt at the audition. Why am I just now making these discoveries? I'd consider firing the screenwriter if it hadn't been me. Once I decided I couldn't use what I had, I worked on a rewrite of the dialogue and planned on a future reshoot. We wrapped the yard shoot and packed up for my cousin's apartment. This is where we staged the evening keg party where Rick and Rod talk about their future plans. When we planned the shoot, I asked my almost college aged cousin and girlfriend to invite all the kids they could to fill out the room. I rented an empty beer keg and supplied cases of beer for drinking.

Disappointingly, only about a dozen showed up. Once again, improvisation rules and you change your vision to coincide with reality. The whole shooting plan I had was thrown out the window. I created a choreography of movements for the 12 people to give the viewer an illusion of more. I worked out the new plan on paper, then executed it. I can't stress enough about staying flexible and adaptive because rarely do things go as planned.

Saturday, September 27

The Dennis Parker scene with my friend Joe Bendavid as Dennis. Joe had exhibited an inclination to play a guy who could talk on and on ponderously, and he did not disappoint. He was so perfect that I blew two of the takes because I laughed loudly enough to be heard by the microphone. What was so funny was the ad lib Joe threw in to keep the stream of consciousness going. Joe was actually waxing on about his son who he had been in many disagreements with recently. Here he was sharing his real-life frustrations out loud: how his son couldn't get a good job and had decided to move in with a bimbo. Bust your gut funny. After getting a successful take, we moved outside to film the subsequent scene to this, which is where Rick gets a parking ticket because of Dennis's soliloquy. We were fortunate enough to have a two hour parking sign outside the offices, which is where we parked Rick's car. I installed a scrap piece of paper under the wipers to double as a parking ticket. Joe saw this and stops me. He told me he got a real parking ticket yesterday, which was in his car. How good was this—I could use a real ticket as a prop. Another fortuitous, serendipitous moment. There would be more to come.

6

Porn Shop Shoot

Prior to Sunday's shoot, I had scouted far and wide for the unlikeliest combination of a porn shop with a pay phone outside. I found that in Warwick, R.I., with the added bonus of it being a stand-alone building, which necessarily tied in with the script, and the bonus of affording us some privacy.

This was a needle in a haystack find, yet it happened. Our luck just kept getting made. The store manager told me I would have to get an okay to shoot from their headquarters a few miles away. He gave me the address and the operations manager's name. I was told that this was the largest retail chain of pornographic products in New England. I drove to the building where I found a gated, pink stucco, two-floor mansion styled building with no signage. I walked into a palatial entryway which very much resembled Larry Flynt's headquarters as depicted in the movie *Private Parts*.

The receptionist greeted me and I asked for the operations manager by name. She asked me very curiously why I wanted to see him. I suspect the receptionist's guarded inquiry was due to the fate that befell Flynt. I told her I was a filmmaker and wanted to see the operations manager. She told me they didn't buy films directly from filmmakers. I explained that I wasn't selling a film, but wanted to shoot a scene in one of their stores. She called the manager and he agreed to see me.

An assistant came for me and walked me to his office. As we walked to his office I was struck by the extremely tasteful interior decorations. Not a nude painting or picture on the walls. There was only antique furniture, Persian rugs, and scenic oil paintings. I was ushered into his office where I was welcomed. I showed him the pages of my script which I planned to film inside and outside his store. He was amused. He gave me his approval and arranged for the store manager to allow us into the store Sunday morning before they opened.

Sunday, September 28

We arrived at the porn shop two hours earlier than we were to go in, shooting the 'beside the road' scene at the phone booth. This is where Rick locks his keys in the car and has to call his office to get a spare set of keys while dodging the details of the location. I suspected that eight o'clock on a Sunday morning in a porn shop parking lot would be a pretty quiet place and I was correct. After shooting those scenes, we took practically no time setting up inside the store, shooting MOS as this scene was intended to have Rick's voice over. Ultimately in post sound, the mixers added the sounds of a couple screwing, which gives the viewer the impression that an X-rated video is playing in the store. Great touch.

From there we drove to an industrial office park and shot the scene where Bob Wish and Rick had a heart-to-heart talk about their relationships. This scene was scripted to take place while they were driving. But as I said before, with a nonexistent budget, a moving car shot was out of the question, so they were shot talking in the car while eating their lunch. Another adlibbed, improvised scene. A change of clothes and another car interior talking scene which takes place on another day in the film is wrapped; this turned out to be a tough day for the actors because of all the dialogue that was contained. Once again, my cast did a great job.

Once these scenes were completed, we returned to the porn shop. I needed to have an establishing scene to open the porn shop sequence, and the morning light was very unflattering at the hour we were there. We shot the exterior establishing scene in the afternoon light, which was photographically better.

From there, we traveled a mile south to a very quiet stretch of road to shoot the supposed rural setting for the porn shop in the context of the film. An easy shoot that wrapped on a very busy Sunday; almost two rolls of film were shot that day.

Saturday, October 4

A day of shooting at Crystal Thermoplastics. We started the day with a shot of Bob and Rick driving toward us in the industrial park, which establishes them going on a sales call together. For my next shot, I double-faced taped my new company sign to the side of the building. A sign with a long story.

First, I needed to come up with a company name of the fictional firm in my movie. I wrote to the Fiber Box Association and requested a directory of all box plants in the United States. After a fruitless search, we came upon the name Ace Box.

Why…1) because it wasn't in use, 2) because it was a great inside joke; it's my lead actor's stage name and nickname, Ace.

I had a sign made out of plastic sheeting that was sprayed with the material that resembles masonry. The lettering was applied by a sign company. The sign was double-faced sticky taped to the Crystal Thermoplastics building which had a masonry façade. Once in place, it looked like the sign was already there. We took some publicity photos and then shot the establishing shot for the movie.

The next shot took place inside where Rick sees Bob Wish, who tells him about the new girl in accounting. The following scene to be filmed is Rick visiting a prospect named Roger, the uninterested prospect who plays solitaire on his computer during Rick's insecure first sales call. We followed that scene by filming the one where Rick is exiting the building and going to his car and then the scene where Rick is driving his car on the road.

I now have only ten seconds worth of film left in the camera so I use it to shoot a sign that warns of surveillance equipment monitoring a parking lot. I wasn't sure if I would use that over another sign for the peeing in the bushes scene, but ten seconds worth of film couldn't be used for anything else. Another good, productive, and efficient day of shooting was in the can.

October 12

We returned to my neighbor Shirley's backyard. We came to re-stage and re-shoot the close-up between Rick and his grandmother, necessary for two reasons… 1) Shirley was looking very admirably at the grandmother as she delivered her lines, which ruined the scene and 2) my original writing was ponderous and bothered me too much. Due to these being close-ups, actors and extras weren't needed thankfully.

Rick and his grandmother were dressed as they were during the party scene. We reshot the new dialogue scenes in close-up, which cut in nicely with the original scenes. Once we were satisfied that we got the shot right, we headed north to Pawtucket, Rhode Island, a city with many old mill buildings.

Northeast Knitting was our destination where I had planned to do some filming both inside and out. David Lavoie, the owner of Northeast Knitting, is a customer and friend of mine. The owner was very gracious in letting us shoot in and around his building. In the neighborhood, there was an abandoned building that lent itself to the montage scenes. This is the point where Rick realizes the desperation of his job, which was finding prospects in this wasteland of decrepit industrial buildings. We also filmed the scene in which Rick hobbles across the street holding his pee and the eventual long release of said pee in the bushes.

Before moving inside for the rest of the shoot, we shot the camera surveillance sign and Rick's reaction to it. Next, we moved inside for the filming of the scene where Rick gets turned away by a receptionist from seeing the purchasing agent and also being denied the use of a restroom. The scene in the elevator is where Rick is holding his bladder, shaking from it, as it makes a sudden stop. We added this scene to the script as we were carting equipment up the elevator. We knew the freight elevator jamming on the way down would be hysterical. So funny, in fact, that I couldn't direct it by watching it. I kept laughing out loud so much that I ruined the takes. I just couldn't direct the scene. So, I ended up directing it from only what I heard. I turned around so I couldn't see Ace shaking from holding the pee. Only his voice could be heard, but his moaning and groaning was challenge enough for my inclination to bust out laughing. We knew we had accomplished our objective when we all had tears in our eyes from laughing.

We then moved upstairs to their reception area. We were now ready to film the scene where

Rick asks the receptionist for the buyers name and then for the use of the men's room. Carol Reavy played the receptionist and brought an Elaine from Seinfeld detached attitude to the part. The fact that she was chewing gum actively as she addressed Rick added so much to her aloofness. After completing that shot we shot another receptionist rejection scene using David Lavoie's wife at a different desk. We planned to keep this as stock footage to use in a montage scene. Unfortunately, we were at the tail end of the roll and the film ran out. Once we completed shooting a roll of film, we would not load another roll unless we knew we were going to shoot it all in the same day or two.

7

The Antagonist Is Ready

Saturday, October 18

Finally, mid-October arrived and Elliott Cohan, the actor portraying my antagonist Edward Cox II, was now free to work with. Prior to committing to me, he had contracted to a Tennessee Williams' monologue play, which occupied his schedule from summer through mid-October. There was so much I needed to shoot with him and I could not wait to start. Once he was available though, he was very specific as to his availability. Blocks of a couple hours per day here and there was his limit. I didn't ask if this was his personal way of working or if he was busy personally, I was just glad to have him.

The first shot comprised no dialogue; it contained only Edward seeing Rick leaving Bonnie's office. The balance of shooting was all the scenes late in the film where Rick and Edward face-off. That was it for scheduled shooting for Edward Cox's character for that weekend.

Sunday, October 19

The shoot that day was in New Bedford, Massachusetts, at Skips Marine's offices, owned by Ray Drouin, a personal friend and customer. His father's office in the building had an ethnically enough look that it was ideal for the Vince Vega character. Vince was played by Carl Ruggerio. Though I had given him instructions to get to Skips Marine, Carl arrived in New Bedford, got lost, and promptly returned home to Providence, 45 minutes away. Meanwhile, I was all set up to shoot and sweating because the office was opened on a Sunday for us to shoot and one of the two actors was absent.

Ray's daughter Heather was cast as the receptionist, so we busied ourselves getting the establishing shot while police searched for Carl Ruggerio. We finally contacted him at home where we gave him his new directions and he came right back to the location. This scene was too funny to shoot, and once again, I had to fight the urge to laugh as he spoke his lines. Some of the lines were things that were said to me by a customer years ago. There's always an inspiration somewhere. The lines were fascinating, racist, and curiously funny all at the same time. All the observers in the room cracked up laughing as soon as I called cut.

This is one of the aspects of filmmaking that is most memorable, the camaraderie and togetherness of a shared experience, laughing and working with new friends and associates. I reminded myself that this was the greatest thing I had ever done.

Saturday, October 25

We returned back to Crystal Thermoplastics and the day started with the receptionist shots in the lobby with Sherry Qualia. From there we went to the conference room shots. This was one of the days that Ace floored us with his ability to be prepared for a day of shooting that spanned from early in the story to late, with several cast members, different frames of mind, and not blowing his lines or requiring many takes. A truly talented guy. I thanked my lucky stars again for picking him. He worked like a dog and always rose to the occasion. The cost of film savings was immeasurable.

The next scene to be filmed was the one with

the salesmen around the table which had, by far, the most characters with dialogue that I'd had in any one scene. I had built a dolly car from a wheeled box frame cart, a true mother of invention kind of vehicle. I bolted a plywood bed on the altered frame and had a machine shop create brackets that I designed to lock the tripod on. The dolly worked, but only on the smoothest of surfaces.

The scene opening is one of the few successful dolly shots to be found in the film. I'm very happy and proud of it, although a distributor, upon seeing my film, asked why I didn't have any cool camera moves in the movie. I answered that I did have a sense of where I would have used fancy camera moves throughout the movie. I used them very sparingly due to the increased film costs because you needed several takes to be sure you captured a good one. Having many camera moves would be a luxury for a film with a non-existent budget. Life can be so unfair.

Back to the scene though, which was an enjoyable shoot. The guys that played the salesmen were a scream. They all had had time to absorb their characters, so they were able to come up with funny ad-libs when Edward Cox II asked them individually what they each could do to increase their sales.

Pretty boy Frank Casters replied, "I do much

better in person, but I suppose I could make some phone calls."

Health food nut Lester Butts answers, "If you could peel off a couple of bucks, I could buy some bran muffins, people like them."

I just about fell over when Sam Babbitt delivered his ad-libbed line. I had, unfortunately, blown too many takes by laughing out loud up until then. I was making mental notes of wasted film and money with each reshoot. I had to adjust my directing approach by biting down on my tongue on subsequent takes. In the case of this scene, everybody cracked up, requiring another take. Another telling example of the excellence of my cast.

8

The Nose Picker Is Found

Saturday, October 26

The scene that I expected would challenge my cast on different levels was The Nose Picking Scene. The scene was inspired by actual events I experienced in my work life. I've met people in my sales visits where the person was picking his nose, or scratching their butt, before extending their hand for a welcome shake. I was always incredulous at their lack of self-awareness. In the weeks leading up to shooting that scene, I spoke to several friends that I thought would be potentially good as the nose picker. He emerged in the form of Peter Colt, a friend I'd made in the Army Reserves. Peter is a Captain and a huge movie buff. He'd started a new job that prevented him from assisting in the making of the movie but he was happy to be cast as a nose picker. With his short hair and serious looks, I knew he was ideal for the role, and he was.

The scene was shot in another office at Crystal Thermoplastics that hadn't been used before. It was a blessing to have so many offices under one roof. I introduced Peter to Ace where they chuckled and joked about the subject matter about to be filmed. Ace asked Peter if he'd sanitized his nose before we rolled. Peter obliged by using several Kleenex tissues to thoroughly swab his nose before shooting began. The scene plays out with Rick sitting across from Peter in a meeting. Rick is making his sales pitch, while Peter sits listening, while subconsciously picking his nose. At the end of Rick's pitch, Peter says he'll consider what was pitched, thanks Rick for stopping by, and extends his nose picking hand for a closing hand shake. Rick gulps as he faces the inevitable, reluctantly extending his hand in this trapped situation. We shot several takes looking for variations in expressions. The timing and pacing of the camera pan was something I decided on and did not deviate. I thought it was effective, always getting a big laugh.

The next scene to film was Rick in the office with Dave the big guy who sponges meals from salesmen. Carl Roggerio who played Dave was perfect. He had the jovial quality that made his character endearing. We were now finished at Crystal Thermoplastics, so we moved down the street where we quickly grabbed a shot of Rick leaving the nose picker's office. This insert was to complete the nose picker sequence. We found an office building we could use, where the company name could be selectively cropped from the shot.

As scripted, Rick was to exit the building with a look of disgust, wiping his hand on his pants. That was until the ever present, quick minded Ace noticed a rag on the base of the stairs and used it to further clean his hands. Great symbolism, Rick was so repulsed that he'd use a rag of questionable origin to clean his hands of the nose picker's germs. Comedic genius.

From there, we went to shoot the scene of Dave and Rick talking in the car. Once the dialogue scenes were completed, we moved to the scene where Dave enters and exits the car at the bank. The Dave character was written to be an enormous guy, but he wasn't in real life. Just to create the illusion or to carry this concept through, I asked Carl to waddle when he walked. It turned out that he really did naturally walk with a waddle that all of us in the crew found hysterical.

We moved down the street to film a similar exit and enter scene at what was to be a shoe repair shop in the movie, but which was really a dry cleaner shop in real life. Selective cropping again eliminated any telltale references to a dry cleaner. Note the pace of Carl's stride in that scene. Funny or what? This was shot M.O.S. and I was glad because I laughed uncontrollably throughout the take.

From there a change of clothes for Dave and back to the bank for the end of the movie montage showing that, although it's a different day, some things never change. All the previous shots were for the earlier Dave montage, which took place on the same day.

Saturday, November 1

This was our first time shooting inside the office building named the Packet Building in downtown Providence, Rhode Island. This was the office of Sharad Batia, an attorney friend of Joe Bendavid's, who graciously offered the use of his office. I scheduled all the scenes in which Edward Cox introduces Rick to all the salesman there. I scheduled all the guys in a rotational order so there'd be a minimum of wasted hanging around time. Since I wasn't paying people, I didn't want to make it a laborious experience. I attempted to be as considerate as possible.

The scenes all involved Edward voicing his enthusiasm for the two guys who were clearly the odd ducks in the organization. Yet the straight, squared-away guy was clearly not the favorite of Edward Cox. The fun part of the shoot was the improvisation of the scene where Edward introduces Lester Butts (Sam Babbitt). We set it up that Edward and Lester were on the sofa talking and after the introductions, Rick sat down between them where the banter between Edward and Lester had Rick's head turning left and right nonstop resembling a tennis balls travel. Another great improv moment that was totally unplanned.

That finished the shooting at the Packet Building. We packed up and headed up to Crystal Thermoplastics for the shots of Rick running into Ann in the hallway, with her talking to Rick in the conference room about fraternization. Once done, we shot the scene at the end of the picture where Rick walks down the hall and goes into Edward's office. This required Ace to change his suit.

A note about costumes: everyone kept track of their clothes for given days in the story, which unburdened me from keeping track. I explained this to each of the actors when they were cast. Not having a costume department requires you to delegate the miscellaneous responsibilities around. There is only one continuity costume issue in the movie, and I don't want to point it out.

9

Life Imitates Art Or Vice Versa

Sunday, November 2

A very big day was planned. Carl Roggerio, who played Dave, was a friend of the owners of Mediterraneo Restaurant in Providence on Federal Hill. Carl arranged with the owner to open the doors for us at 9 a.m.. But some wires were crossed and we didn't have anyone to open for us until 11 a.m.. I felt a stab of panic; the guy had to show up soon or I'd be substituting stills in the movie. We all sat in our cars outside till the cook arrived at 11 a.m.. We (actors, crew, and extras) piled in and got to work setting up.

The scene shot at Mediterraneo was about Dave, the buyer, who wants porn magazines from Rick. Well, when we were setting up the lights and putting extras in place, I noticed that the kitchen, which is in the background of the shot, was visible and it looked uninhabited. I asked the cook who let us in to please move around in the background during the shooting to add realism. I found him obscured behind a refrigerator reading a porn magazine; I startled him as he put the magazine down nonchalantly. He had no idea that was the subject matter of the scene. Life imitates art or vice versa. I was pressed for time because our next shooting location was at 2 p.m. at Action Container in Pawtucket, Rhode Island, approximately15 minutes away.

The owner Glen Gardiner of Action is a friend of mine. He also happened to be a competitor that I felt more comfortable with asking to use his factory instead of my own. This is a telling sign of how I viewed and considered the people I worked for.

I now had to set up, rehearse, shoot the scenes and assorted coverage, tear down, and be at Action Container in three hours. I had to be fast, really fast. I had worked out a revised shooting schedule while sitting in the car waiting for the doors to open. The longer I waited, the more abbreviated or condensed the shot list became. Also in the car with me was Damon Hartley, a wonderful actor from the Newport Playhouse, who I cast based on seeing him in other plays. I knew he'd be great as the waiter that plays off the Dave character in the restaurant.

Damon didn't have a car, so he rode with me up to Mediterraneo, and I would drop him off at the bus station for his return trip home. After dropping Damon Hartley off, we would have to race to Action Container to shoot the scenes in the sample room. Action Container's owner, as I mentioned, was kind enough to not only let me shoot box plant scenes but also open their plant to me on a Sunday at 2 p.m.. Hence the reason why I was not going to be late for the shoot.

Having this pressure on me and having only a few hours to shoot forced me to consolidate my shot list and omit close-ups. A decision that ultimately compromised the rhythm of the scene in which Dave bragged about his war-time lover and how she pleasured him. Irene Wolansky, the actor who played the lady listening in on Dave's conversation, was not told of the subject matter. I just wanted to capture her reaction and surprise in the scene spontaneously. We ran a few other takes, but ultimately used the first one in the movie. I regret that I failed to get a close-up of her reaction to Dave's reminiscing of the sexual encounter with his Vietnamese lover.

Close up reaction shots are a staple of comedy and I overlooked it in my haste. So much for my insistence in compromise for economic sense.

Speaking of Dave's scene, the dialogue spoken, which was sexually explicit, was a concern for my sister because my nephew Dave was the sound man and he was 13-years-old. My niece was 16, so my sister asked if I could substitute my niece on sound and send my nephew to the car for the scene. I did just that and Dave, my nephew, wasn't pleased at all. But hey, it was Mom's request. I'm only the enforcer. Was he ever bummed.

We hastily tore down and headed to Action Container for our sample room shoot. Elliott Cohan (Edward Cox) and Neil Santoro (Steve) were arriving and were greeted by the owners Gail, Gary, and Glen. We set up the camera and lights so that there would be a minimum of movement for expedience sake. I reviewed the schedule and determined where all the camera angles would be used. I determined that Elliott's shots would be done first as they were the briefest of all that were planned. Once Elliott's were shot, we settled in on the longer, more dialogue intensive scene between Ace (Rick) and Neil Santoro (Steve). During the dry run rehearsals, Neil was hitting some snags in the dialogue. Then when we shot the scene, his problems came at a different place. As we were rolling more film and I was amassing unfinished takes at a cost I didn't want to think about, it was time for a new strategy. I decided to move the camera and create a cut with a new camera angle from which to resume the dialogue. This is the only way to intercut the continuation of the scene, without the disruption of a jump cut, which would pull the viewer out of the scene.

A short explanation about jump cuts. A jump cut is where the camera angle doesn't change but there's a distinct cut with the dialogue continuing. The person on screen is usually not in the same exact position so you see it and feel the unnaturalness. This can and is used artistically for effect, but in my case, it wasn't an option as I'm not a fan of the jump cut.

Several takes and camera moves later, we had it all in the can. I thanked the owners of Action Container and we packed up for home. Another good weekend of shooting was wrapped.

Every Monday morning, I packaged up my film and Fedex'd it overnight to Du-Art Labs in New York where the film was processed and transferred to Beta SP with key codes and time codes applied. This was the way I was instructed to have everything done by Tom Ohanian, my editor. I also ordered a super VHS copy for my own personal evaluation. When the processed film and cassettes arrived, I anxiously reviewed the silent S-VHS cassette to confirm I had what I expected on film. My only re-shoots for the whole film was the shoot in Shirley's yard when she was looking at Ethel the grandmother proudly and my poorly lit scene in Jane Pickens Theater in which the scene didn't look like a theater would when a film is showing.

Tuesday Night, November 4

It was our one and only Wednesday shoot, only because Elliott (Edward Cox) was available and Sharad Batia's office was as well. We'd moved into the office and the ever-ready Elliott banged out the two scenes, back to back, which took place on different days in the film. A real pro. His availability was a scheduling problem but his preparation was dead on. It was a real pleasure to work with him. His reaction shots on the phone were impressive, coupled with a slow lens zoom to accentuate the impact. My friend Marie Iriye was on the opposite end of the phone in another office reciting the lines that would be later dubbed by another person. The pacing of the words she spoke had to be similar to the ones that would be dubbed in later. My friend Brown Beazer, who has an authoritative voice, would be the voice the film viewer would hear. I was feeling more and more confident in getting the film finished. Trying like hell not to dwell on negatives or the reality of my longshot chances that I'd have a credible film when I was done.

Friday Night, November 7

We returned to Action Container to film the scene where Rick and Steve are in the sample room. A smooth shoot that hopefully wouldn't interrupt the lives of our hosts too much. That night, I called around for extras to be in the background of the scene in the bar at Davenport's that we'd be filming the next morning. I got several maybes. Maybes worried me.

10

Drinking Beers At 10 Am

Saturday, November 8

We arrived early at Davenport's restaurant and Greg Davenport was there early to greet us. While we awaited our 'maybe' extras, we shot the establishing scene where Rod (Gerard Marzilli) and Rick (Ace Aceto) arrived and entered Davenport's restaurant early in the film, which chronologically took place soon after their college graduation in June. Davenport's entrance is now decorated for Thanksgiving (cornstalks adorned the entire entryway and could not easily be removed). Selective composing again eliminated the cornstalks on the left and right sides of the frame. Inside we shot the scene where Rick and Rod discussed the trials and tribulations of love and career. Above the bar where they sit is a chalkboard listing the drinks of the day. Pumpkin flavored ales and drawings of pumpkins are all around. Needless to say, we avoided any wide establishing shots. Besides, the big number of maybe extras didn't materialize, so we didn't need to see this empty bar at 10 a.m.. Three guys did show up, so we planted them directly behind our actors on the frontal shots. Greg Davenport poured everyone a beer for the sake of authenticity. Ace and Rod were awesome. No blown lines, solid preparation, just a couple of dry runs and they were off. With their preparation, tons of money was saved. Good actors can save money and a movie. Concepts you don't appreciate until you're in it. From there, we had only the scene with Rick calling his girlfriend Kathy from a phone booth.

My weekly scouting trips located a lone payphone in a deserted section of town that helped me once again in avoiding crowd control or the need for extras for authenticity. The fact that I didn't have extras was a minor concern.

You can only deal with so much improvising when you're understaffed. So, I chose my battles and this one wasn't that important. Shooting this scene concluded our day as I had a problem coordinating any other actors and locations for the day. A free weekend afternoon off was an uncommon event, half of me welcomed it, and the other half felt guilty because I wasn't able to shoot the whole day; I viewed it as a lost opportunity.

Sunday, November 9

This was a shoot at my brother-in-law's office. First on deck was the scene where the egotistical salesman, Frank Casters, counsels the rookie Rick in his car outside a prospect's office. My brother-in-law was the new owner of a Mercedes-Benz so I naturally asked to use it for Frank's car… a made to order prop.

For the next shot, we moved inside where Frank asked the receptionist to see the purchasing agent. My girlfriend Carol Kent was recruited for the role of the receptionist. Tight quarters in the office necessitated me to shoehorn myself into a corner of the room with the viewfinder and my head jammed into the corner to get the shot wide enough to take in Rick sitting in the chair reacting to Frank Castor admiring himself in the mirror. Fun and funny but physically painful to shoot.

The last scene was in Jeff Lerner's office, another friend of Ace Aceto, who we knew could pull off the indifferent attitude we were looking for. The scene depicted the cocky Frank Casters pitching the purchasing agent while Rick's voice-over (VO) overdubs Frank's rambling. I told Frank to just ramble on with a sales pitch and eat up screen time for a specific amount of seconds, sufficient time for Rick's voiceover to overdub. He told me he didn't know what a sales pitch was. Of course not, he's not a salesman. But I am, so I wrote a bunch of soundbites on Post-it notes and stuck them all around the desktop out of camera view so that his head could roam, yet find stuff to say. It worked just great. He segued from one Post-it note to the next fluidly. Another obstacle had been overcome.

We wrapped around noon and packed up for the biggest shoot in the movie, the movie theater scene. It was logistically the biggest because I was able to use our local Jane Pickens movie theater in Newport, Rhode Island. The Jane Pickens shows independent films. A great and classic movie theater featuring a balcony and proscenium. It was also the biggest shoot because of all the extras needed to make it look believable. I called everyone I knew except people I'd already used as extras.

This was the only scene that I had actually storyboarded. My camera operator Guy Weston was caught by surprise when I pulled it out of left field on him; a nice, funny moment between us. He understood the rhythm of what I was trying to achieve visually after going over it. The only potential problem with this shoot was a major one. I wasn't a hundred percent sure of how to light the scene to make it look real. I took an estimated guess and lost. When the processed film came back, I knew I had failed. I truly couldn't live with the footage, so I had to borrow the theater again and call everyone back for the reshoot. Of course, not all of them could make the reshoot, so I felt even worse. Several disappointed extras who would not make it to the silver screen. If you use an inexperienced cinematographer, be prepared for these kind of results.

The second attempt was successful and we were relieved it was now behind us. My production planning showed that due to countless factors, we would be down for two weeks. My crew and I needed some down time.

11

Billie Price Being Billie Price

Saturday, November 22

I just knew this would be a fun shoot. The morning shoot would be with Billy Price played by Billy Price. All shots would be at a customer's of mine, Enviropack. Billy Price is an acquaintance from my Army Reserve unit. He was a Sergeant Major and a natural comic without trying. One day at Reserves, he was relating a story to Guy Weston, who became my camera operator. As I overheard this tale, I was cracking up. Billy's style of speech, cadence, and delivery is unique and very him. It was right there and then that I decided to write him in. Billy is African American and he can always find a racial slant to everything, so I knew I had to capitalize on his strengths and worldview.

I decided to create a new character for my screenplay. An African American named Billy Price who owns a black hair care business. He is pissed off that his race is underrepresented in the sales field. His experience is that he rarely, if ever, sees a Black salesman. Billy only comes out to meet Ricky Williams because the name sounds African American. He is sadly disappointed to discover he's another white sales guy.

Ironically, my protagonist's name is Ricky Williams, the same name as the Heisman trophy winning running back that very same year. Serendipity? How perfect was this set up? I also knew that it needed to be a running gag because it would be that funny.

Altogether, four scenes that Billy and Ace would be in would all be shot that one morning. This would require four changes in clothing to indicate four different days. If I had had a wardrobe department, I'd have dressed Billy in dated suits. Luck was again on my side, Billy showed up with four dated suits. How good is this? Well, he didn't actually show up, I picked him up. Billy doesn't have a car, so he gave me directions to his apartment in Providence. Only in Rhode Island could this happen, he lives two blocks from Terry Leander who plays Bonnie. Another sign or omen I think.

Filming the Billy Price scenes were a pleasure and a treat. I allowed Billy to improvise, and did he ever. In the close-up shot where the very white Rick asks Billy if he'd like to buy boxes, Billy shakes his head side to side and rolls off this "NNNOOOOO!" All of us cracked up, resulting in a lost take. We reshot and got it, but the entire crew had their hands over their mouths, muffling their laughter. Ditto for me and the addition of tears coming down my face.

He did the same to us all again when we shot the scene when Rick brings him a display box and asks him if he would be "interested in something like this?" To which Billy ad-lib an innovative, "you best be stepping," as he pushed Rick out of frame and totally off-screen. It was an indescribably hysterical ad-libbed moment. That line, "you best be stepping," was a treasure. The payoff at the end of the movie is that a Black salesman would eventually be hired by the box company to service Billy Price's company.

Guy Weston, my camera operator, had two acquaintances in his church that he felt would be good candidates for the female receptionist, who was in all of those scenes, and the young Black man that would ultimately get hired as a salesman for the end of the movie. The young salesman's scene was shot M.O.S. so there was no problem with dialogue there. When we rehearsed the scene in which Rick asks the female receptionist what the company manufactures, her line was scripted to read, "we make Black hair care products." She didn't like the line and asked to change it to, "ethnic hair care products." The only problem was, in rehearsal, it became a tongue twister for her and she could not consistently get it out, so we went back to, "Black hair care products." Hey, I did try to be accommodating.

We wrapped this location and set off a few miles to meet with Sam Babbitt (Lester Butz) to shoot a pickup shot of Rick and Lester getting in their car, which was to be shot in an industrial park. We needed to kill some time as the rest of the day would be at the Eggs Up Restaurant starting at 2 p.m., which was the time that this breakfast-only restaurant closed daily. The owner Bob invited his off-shift employees and friends to serve as extras. This was one of the best attended extra castings for the whole film. We were able to get two-sided coverage of Rick and Lester coming into this supposedly old haunt of Lester's. Lester's daily diet dialogue in these scenes was so funny that the entire restaurant cracked up on the rehearsals. Everyone roared, including Lester (Sam Babbitt). After a few dry runs, we were all able to contain ourselves long enough to get the shots.

Ace took this scene as an opportunity to break down the fourth wall. The fourth wall is the invisible space between the actors and an audience. When an actor breaks down the fourth wall, they are, in effect, directly interacting with the audience. Ace does this by looking at the audience and shaking his head back and forth in disbelief as the Lester character waxes on about his eating healthy in service of "clean bowels." This addition to the scene gave it a little more punch and a wink, wink to the viewer. Everything went great except—and a very big except—we underestimated the ambient sound of the air-conditioning system.

The system created a steady drone throughout the entire soundtrack. I later learned in post-production how ugly the repair choices would become. The sound editors applied a digital audio technology entitled noise shaping. Noise shaping removes some of the background noise but has a negative effect on the rest of the soundtrack, which is the dialogue. They did this and it helped, but the entire scene has a different audible sound than the rest of the movie. The low-level drone is there. The only alternative, other than a re-shoot, was to use ADR, which is automated dialogue replacement. This involves bringing the actors into a studio and having them read their lines in sync with their lips on screen. ADR is very time-consuming, hence costly. I ended up taking the cheapest way out. Noise shaping left me with a less than ideal scene, but a saving of hundreds of dollars.

12

Snow In Summer

Sunday, November 23

We were at Fisher's Farm stand, and it was snowing. The scene there was where Rick stopped to ask a deaf farmer if he would be interested in buying boxes from him. Luck was on my side once again as we had a room full of employees bagging squash for stores for Thanksgiving, which was only four days away…great for the establishing shot. This was the busiest time of year and the only time they work on weekends.

I cast an actor named Arnie Green as the farmer. The real farmer, Mr. Fisher, I had cast as an extra. I gave Mr. Fisher a line to deliver on cue but his timing was off on all the rehearsals. I primed him once again and then rolled the camera. His timing was a little better when filmed on camera, and I deemed it was an adequate enough take. Frustratingly off, but good enough.

We then shot the office scene M.O.S., where loud rock music would dominate the scene. My prior scouting visit led me to this tiny claustrophobic office that was difficult to light. I just decided to go with a frontal light and be done with it. You've got to pick your battles as I've said before. The last two scenes to film here were of Rick arriving and then leaving. It was drizzling on the snow. We wrapped and headed 30 miles north to Lincoln, Rhode Island, which is where we would shoot Rick and Lester talking in the car. We arrived at the appointed rendezvous, McDonald's for coffee and a conference on how we would shoot the scenes. We dry ran the dialogue while surveying the improving weather outside. The rain stopped, so we headed over to the industrial park where we found snow-covered ground and trees. The site I choose to shoot at had evergreen trees in the background, which were now solid white with snow. The reason the snow is a problem is because this scene takes place just after Rick's graduation from college in June. The month of June and snow just don't go together. My nephew, Dave, the sound man, took a broom and proceeded to sweep the grass and trees that were visible in the background of the shot. It took him a half hour to do. I spent the time setting up and rehearsing. I stuck the camera just outside the driver's window, and composed by zooming on Rick and Lester. Once composed, I directed my nephew Dave to clear any of the snow that I could see in the viewfinder. I asked him to go a little beyond, knowing that the viewfinder is not a hundred percent accurate. We shot the scenes uneventfully but found in the processed images that there was snow visible in the right corner of the frame. Damn, but it was so subtle that no one had picked up on it except me, and now you, that you've read this.

To round out the day, we returned to Crystal Thermoplastics to shoot the scene where Rick and Bob visited Pete, the buyer, who was set up with a hooker by Bob. Pete was to be played by T. J. Curran. I found T. J. on the night I watched my first audition at City Nights dinner theater in Pawtucket, Rhode Island. He auditioned that night and when he was on stage, he removed his trousers and sat down on the provided sofa reading his lines, without a change in his dialogue. I assumed that that's what was called for in the script.

When he finished his read, the director Ernie Medeiros asked him why he removed his pants. T.J.'s reply was, "I personally know guys like this character and they're Guidos who wouldn't want to wrinkle their pants when sitting at home."

You have to love someone with that much insight. I had cast T. J. in my mind at that moment. So there we were, shooting him in the character I envisioned that day. He was a perfect fit in the role. A college student at URI, yet he looked like he was in his thirties. He also happened to be a theater major. He melted right into the part. I didn't use many reaction shots in close-up, but did here because it helped the scene.

Friday, November 28

The day after Thanksgiving and we were about to film the scene where Rick and Edward have their last showdown and Edward's world comes crashing down around him. This was a scene that I felt warranted close-ups because of its pivotal role in the picture. The audience needed to see Edward's world crumbling.

When we completed the sequence at the Packet Building, we headed up to Woonsocket, Rhode Island. As a homage to *Dumb and Dumber,* I attempted to duplicate the shot where the camera drives past a cluster of old red brick, industrial buildings on River Street that were abandoned. I watched the laser disc of *Dumb and Dumber* at home enough times and made notes as to where the footage started and stopped; that was what I used for the timing of our car.

The shoot went fairly easily. Once we were satisfied, we headed south to shoot Rick pulling into the parking lot of Collyer Wire, a very depressing site. All that was there was an abandoned building with a parking lot growing weeds through the cracks in the dried out asphalt.

The next scene was a montage consisting of more driving past abandoned, closed down businesses. It is an unfortunate reality in Rhode Island that we have a lot of old abandoned mill buildings. During our whirlwind tour of Rhode Island's best abandoned properties, I found an alley that would drive the point home as to Rick's hopelessness. It was only during rehearsal of the action that we decided to add him calling out, "hello, is anyone here?" with an echo to assimilate the dead space of the alley way around our hero. The scene was part of the montage with voiceover that would show the viewer how hopeless Rick's situation is. The, "hello, is anyone here?" punctuated the voiceover. After completing this scene, which would conclude our montage, we headed to our next and last shoot for the day, or night as it was, downtown Providence, Rhode Island.

13

A Frustrating Night Scene

I scouted the city in preproduction looking for a street with plenty of light for night shooting, When I was scouting for this scene, I had and I did so with two criteria in mind: 1) The light meter had to reflect the value of f /2.8 or better, and 2) I didn't want to have a lot of pedestrian traffic to have to control. The location that I identified passed muster on those two points, but didn't on the two points I hadn't considered: 1) auto and bus traffic was fairly regular, and 2) the wind direction that night directed the air traffic into the Providence airport by flying directly over our heads. The jet engine's roar overhead made you think you were on the runway. Compounding the problem was the low cloud cover, which prevented us from visually anticipating a plane approaching. This location was fraught with problems.

I had also planned to use my custom-made camera dolly for the tracking shot as Rick and Rod talked about this theater experience. Well, the sidewalk had seam imperfections, which caused a hop in the dolly, so we moved the dolly into the street only to find it just as unusable due to road irregularities. The camera bobbed continuously through the dry run, so there was no wasted film. The dolly was a good concept that in practice didn't work unless you were on a carpet, which worked on the sales meeting scene and a minor move in the restaurant scene where Rick and Bonnie discussed the office manager's warning about fraternization.

Back to the scene. We had all these problems, buses and cars going by or low flying passenger jets in the fog overhead ruining the sound. We did our best to time our shooting when cars and buses were stopped at the traffic light down the road. We still couldn't anticipate the overhead planes, so every take that night required a bit of mathematical probability and Murphy's Law thrown in.

It goes without saying that we blew a lot of takes that night. The scene was written for Rick and Rod to be discussing their lives while walking home from the theater. Now that we could not use the dolly, I was forced to use the zoom lens in lieu of. The camera was on sticks (tripod) and the lens zoomed as the two guys approached. The sound guy, Dave, walked alongside of them off-frame. The conditions forced it to evolve into a long take that necessitated the actors to speak the dialogue of the entire scene in one take, which they both did beautifully.

The other variable wasn't as easy…timing the long takes between passing traffic and planes. We would start the take as soon as the light down the street turned red and hoped we would be done before the cars took off on the green and arrived next to us. We were all fired up when Rick uttered his last words and gave the shake of his head to end the scene just before the sound of traffic entered the mike on the final last take. It was as close to perfect timing as we were ever going to get.

The week before, Peter and Bobby Farrelly were filming a scene from *There's Something about Mary* five blocks away from where we were, yet they got the Mayor of Providence, Buddy Cianci, to shut down the buses and the pile driving on the construction for the new Providence Place Mall so as not to interfere with filming. Geez that would've been nice!

I related this story the next year when my film was in the Rhode Island International Film Festival to Carolyn Testa of the RI film and TV Office. She in turn related my story to the Mayor.

He told her he would have shut down South Water Street for me if I had asked. Great! Why do offers for assistance always come in after you need them? Alanis Morissette was right. Here I was thinking I had to shoot guerrilla style when I could have had the Hollywood treatment. Damn. In reality though, I didn't ask in advance because I expected to be hassled with requests for insurance, permits, and God knows what else. It made more sense to me to go in and shoot for two hours and be done with it.

Saturday, November 29

Our location that morning was Saki's Pizza, Cumberland, RI, before it opened its doors for that day's business. We were shooting the scene at the end of the film where Edward loses his job and has taken another as a pizza deliveryman. His Cadillac has a pizza delivery sign attached, which is an interesting contrast. It was another fun shoot with everyone trying to keep a straight face through it all. Rod (Gerard Marzilli) behind the counter, was a picture of resignation, doing what he loathes, as he confessed mid-story. He was now in a management position passing down orders to Edward, the guy we'd grown to accept as the boss in the picture, who was now a delivery guy.

We were able to use the now infamous camera

dolly in this scene after rearranging the throw rugs around the floor of the pizza shop. An unintended goof up that occurred in the shoot was when Elliot exits the pizza shop with the delivery order of boxes that were empty. I reminded him to walk as though there was weight to them. He did just that but when he exited the shop, the wind outside picked up the upper box and tossed it at his car. It was such a funny moment that we left it in as is, rather than edit the scene short of the box toss. We were able to wrap our shoot before the pizza shop opened for business.

From there we headed to Joe and Jane Bendavid's house for the scene in Edward Cox's kitchen. Joe and Jane were away for Thanksgiving, so they left me the key to the house for our use.

14

I Break My Friend's Car Window

Ultimately, Joe and Jane Bendavid and their house are in *BOXedMAN*. Having been to this house socially, I knew the layout both inside and out and knew it would lend itself to the film. All the actors rendezvoused at noon, one hour after we wrapped at Saki's 25 miles away. It appears that my timing and scheduling was pretty well on target. Either that, or I subconsciously hurried every shoot just so that I wouldn't have people waiting for me at the next location. We set up the breakfast scene and did a dry run. Everyone was on the mark. Mary Concannon (Mrs. Cox) is just too good as the wife who is fed up with her jerk husband. The loathing in her voice is scathing.

When we moved outside for the car scene she really got into it. She told me afterward she'd never called anyone an asshole before, but it was scripted that way and she delivered it very naturally. She said it felt quite cathartic.

This scene brought the ugly out of everyone. Edward's character was so despicable that 12-year-old Danielle, a niece of the purchasing agent at Crystal Thermoplastics, ad-libbed her own line during the frantic dragging the boy through the bushes scene. She screams at Elliott, "You're not my father anymore." When we witnessed this scene during the editing, all of us couldn't stop laughing. Just a timely, priceless, touch of improvisation. The entire shoot went fine until we wrapped. We then discovered that the window the boy was hanging from wouldn't come back up. I had the car for the weekend, borrowed from a friend, Frank Toner. Frank lent me his gray Cadillac Coupe DeVille, which personified the Edward Cox character. It was a made to order vehicle for this film. Frank lent the car to me and I had the window in the jammed down position. I still needed the car the next day. I was thankful there was no rain in the weather forecast. I brought the car back home as it was. The next day's shoot was all at Crystal Thermoplastics' offices.

Sunday, November 30

We loaded up the Caddy with all the gear, the entire film crew, and rode in an open air car on a chilly November day for an hour. I had the heat on full blast and we had our jackets all zipped up for good measure. David, who was sitting at the passenger side window attempted to keep the blast of air out by holding up a jacket. It didn't help much. One thing we did have was a group of real troopers. If anything could have created a mutiny, this would have been it.

We arrived at Crystal Thermoplastics and unloaded our gear for the first shoot of the day. The scene was Edward Cox II pulling up to the office after the scene which took place in his driveway with his son. I wanted to carry over the laugh from the previous scene by planting a connective device in the form of twigs and branches sticking out from the corners of his door jams. Hopefully, the viewer wouldn't pick up the fact that the passenger car window was down.

In retrospect, I think the scene would have been funnier if I had gone over the top and used larger branches sticking out from the door jams. I went for realism and used short pieces, which, upon viewing, didn't pack the laugh that it could have been. In fact, I'm not sure you can even detect what they are. These are the kind of things that will haunt a filmmaker forever.

After that shot, we moved indoors to film Rick approaching the receptionist at the beginning of the movie. Sherry Quaglia, a very funny actress, was cast as the receptionist. She had this sarcastic, biting expression without saying a word. She would roll her eyes and shrug her shoulders, which would make you feel so insignificant. She brought along her equally attractive sister as a receptionist for another scene that day. Ace, being single, and put into this environment with two attractive single women was a bit too much, a testosterone and estrogen cocktail that was far too volatile. Between flirting and clowning, it was the only time during the production that I felt a loss of control. Trying to get everyone in a working frame of mind was a task. It was just the wrong ingredients at the wrong time. It was that one occasion which showed me another potential problem that can undermine an independent feature. Loss of control.

The cast members eventually felt my level of frustration and brought themselves under control. By the time we finished filming the scene of Rick approaching Sherry the receptionist, Elliott and Vincent Lupino arrived on schedule. We were to shoot their scene which let the viewer know that Edward Cox, the button-down character, is known by his neighbor as Teddy. This scene exposes the façade of Edward Cox II.

I believe the scene was necessary, but my editor, Tom Ohanian, hated it and felt it served no purpose. I still maintained it was necessary; we deliberated back and forth. Our compromise came about through trimming the scene. At that point it was trimmed to 27 seconds in length and Tom acquiesced.

The next scene to film was Rick arriving at Ace Box for his interview. During preproduction brainstorming meetings, Ace had come up with idea that Rick would own a shit box car, and Ace knew he could borrow one from his friend Doug, the manager of the Comedy Connection in Providence, Rhode Island. It was a faded Audi that had seen better days. It was great and we augmented it with the sound of a run-on engine at the suggestion of Postmaster Sound guys during our spotting session.

We were now down to the last two scenes to shoot that day. The first one was of Sherry Quaglia's sister in the role of a receptionist, which was inserted in the rejection montage. After shooting the scene, we changed offices using the many available ones at the Crystal Thermoplastics' movie set.

The next and last scene to film was where Rick discussed the artwork with David Holder, who I cast because he looked to me like a bohemian, graphic artist, Bob Ross/John Gnagy type. The artwork they discussed is for the fictitious Icy Teas Company, which comes into play as the catalyst that becomes the undoing of the antagonist, Edward Cox II. I was fortunate to have friends in the graphics business as suppliers in my real-life job. They run a company named Die Tech Associates in Randolph, Massachusetts; they were terrific in coming up with an actual logo for Icy Teas to be used in the scene. My gratis IOU list continued to grow.

Completing that scene wrapped our production for another weekend. Once again, we timed the shoot well and finished off the entire roll of film. I now had three rolls of film to send to Du Art Labs from the three-day holiday weekend of shooting. Working on a film in all your free time or days off, including long holiday weekends, without minding that you missed a holiday weekend, really makes you aware of how much you really love the work. Tomorrow, it was back to the day job.

During that following week, Michael Corrente was shooting his new feature film, *Outside Providence,* which was adapted from Peter Farrelly's 80s era novel. The screenplay was written by Peter and Bobby Farrelly and Michael Corrente and starred Alec Baldwin. Bobby Farrelly was on location advising during the shooting and I met both of them at the old armory in Providence, Rhode Island. When I contacted Michael and asked if I could sit in as an observer, he welcomed me with an, "Of course, you're a Rhode Island filmmaker," which gave me a tremendous boost.

I was surprised when I entered the cavernous old armory to find they had erected a full-sized tenement building mock-up with which to film. Boy, did I feel small-time in that environment. I spent an afternoon observing while making small talk with Bobby Farrelly. Bobby was interested in my independent film. The $25,000 budget I quoted was obviously a curiosity to him because he asked several questions about it. He recognized I had no studio deal, and that my film was a thoroughly prospective project. I'm 100% sure he thought I was totally nuts. Bobby did impart a bit of valuable advice. He said that I needed to find that one person of power that believed in my project. A champion of sorts, be it studio executive, distributor, or agent.

He stressed that nothing would happen until that happened. Those words would replay in my head throughout my production. He wished me well when I left and I the same on *There's Something about Mary*. The surprising thing about the goings on behind the scenes on their set versus my set was that there wasn't a difference organizationally; the major difference was the size of the crews. Michael had assistants and assistants to the assistants. Mine was a bare-bones director, sound, camera, script supervisor, period.

Bobby Farrelly was alone because Peter was home impregnating his wife, or so he said. Bobby later said, upon being told that I shot on River Street in Woonsocket as a homage to *Dumb and Dumber,* that he would have given me the shot to use. I have to say once again, why do offers for assistance always come in after you needed them? Alanis Morissette strikes again.

15

The Bottling Plant

Saturday, December 6

That day we'd shoot the Icy Teas stuff. A customer of mine in my day job is a bottling company named R.I. Beverage. The general manager, Bill O'Connell, gave me the okay to shoot in his plant on Saturday morning. I'd spoken to him about it before hand and asked him if any of his plant workers would like to be in the movie. One of his maintenance workers wanted to but asked if he could get time and a half pay because it was a Saturday. We informed him that this was a no-pay shoot, which led him to decline his involvement. Here was a guy with absolutely no Hollywood aspirations. So, I called a friend of mine that owns

Elite Auto Repair and asked him if he'd like to be in the picture. No problem, "love to," replied Jim Paiva. I called a couple of other friends to be the impatient management suits in the scene and they gladly agreed. We, the camera crew, arrived early so that we could play out the shoot. I wanted to use my dolly again, which has seen only two successful uses to date.

Karen Kessel and Ace Aceto arrived and we proceeded to set up the dolly shot. Flat floor, no obstructions...I went for it and shot a good five to six seconds of Karen, Toni the plant manager, arriving at the machine that boxes the bottles. The dolly worked wonderfully in this application but Tom Ohanian, the editor, felt it was too lengthy upon reviewing the shot during editing. He condensed it and was absolutely right to do so; I had used an over enthusiastic application of the underutilized dolly.

Back to the shoot...I set up the actors for the scene by the bottling machine. My friends Tom Scott and Russ Dubuc had the difficult job of standing to the side of the machine, arms folded, looking indifferent and impatient. This scene sets up the turn of events at the end of the movie. Jim Paiva, who played a mechanic in the scene had one line, which was, "Oh, I didn't see that before." This became his mantra throughout the holiday season. Everywhere I saw him socially he'd recite his one line. What a ham. After shooting the scene, Bill O'Connell, the general manager, ran the bottling line so that I had the establishing shot that precedes the dialogue in the movie.

Wrapping there, we moved back to our studio Crystal Thermoplastics, where we shot the Icy Teas office scene with Rick and Toni, the plant manager. The scenes were troublesome to shoot as Karen had difficulties with the lines in a tongue twisting kind of way. We shot this scene from different camera angles, so the mathematical probabilities were becoming apparently astronomical. Some of the scenes were shot eight times, each time with different camera angles, very scary at $35 per minute. In the end, we finally got it and completed our Saturday shoot. I was happy to have enough adequate takes to consider this shoot finished. I was also happy to see that we had run the camera out of film, which is the most perfect way to end the day. No redoing a scene or part of one just to use up the roll of film. I made a practice of not leaving film in the camera waiting for another weekend of shooting.

It was about 3 p.m. and we—being me, Carol, Dave, Guy, and Ace—all go down the street to Saki's Pizza where we shot last month. We ordered two pizzas, eat lunch, and talk about how the day went. It started to snow as we ate, and I get an inspiration to add a new montage scene relating to a farmhouse. Ace seemed to remember a farmhouse, in a pastoral setting a few miles away and if we rushed, we could shoot it before darkness set in.

We gobbled down the pizza, jumped into the cars, and raced behind Ace who is bird-dogging this expedition. We arrived and it was just as he said abandoned, so we didn't have to ask permission. I woke Dave out of a sound sleep in the back seat and tell him to prep the DAT recorder. Ace and I dry run the blocking as Guy prepped the camera. We were all set to go when we made the big discovery, for the second time that day…we were out of film! DUUHHH!!!

What the hell were we all thinking, or not thinking. We were all so tired that we collectively forgot that we had run out of film an hour and a half ago. There we were, in a beautiful farmhouse and field setting, with a gentle snow falling in the failing light, and we couldn't do a damn thing about it. We tore down in the waning light, said our goodbyes, and headed to our homes.

Sunday, December 7

The location was R.J. Carbone, Florist Wholesalers (another customer of mine). That day we'd shoot the nursing home scene. The reception area at the florist supply house could easily double for a nurse's station. Seeing I knew the owners, Steve and Tom Carbone, and didn't know anyone at a hospital or nursing home, made this location scout a no-brainer. The nursing home staff were my camera operator Guy Weston, and the nurse that tells Rick that his grandmother died was played by Jane Bendavid, wife of Joe Bendavid. The only preparation that we needed for this scene was to move signs for florist display sales.

This shoot went easily, thanks once again to Ace, who was prepped as always. We shot as few takes as possible, saving film, money, and time. We wrapped and moved on to Crystal Thermoplastics for the remainder of the day's shooting. On tap was the scene where Rick talks to his manager about the turkey stuffing display that wouldn't stay standing. The plant manager was played by a friend, Bob Friedman. Now comes the moment that I had been both dreading and looking forward to. I cast myself in the role of Nick, the whacked-out customer service manager inspired by the many people I have known that when asked to do something, would spend more time explaining why they couldn't do it, than actually doing the task. It happens all the time. My problem was that I hadn't had time to memorize the dialogue I wrote, so I rehearsed it prior to rolling the camera. The dry runs only confirmed my lack of preparation. The crew was tired, and ready to go home and here I was eating up the clock, practicing my lines futilely. I decided that I needed a cheat sheet, or cue card, with the dialogue on it out of camera view. Well, a two-minute stream of consciousness read from an actual card is harder to do than you might think. I was very aware that my eyes were scanning the words, which would have been foolish looking.

Carol and Guy both suggested I hang it up and pack up for the night or possibly send an actor in. Point well-made, but deep down I still wanted to try the part. I asked that we do a take with me ad-libbing. Roll the camera and I'd ramble like an overworked nutcase. Well, by the time I called cut on my own scene, my nephew Dave, read off the times on the DAT recorder which read almost two minutes. Stream of consciousness sustained just shy of two minutes, but was it any good? The cast and crew were laughing, which could be a good sign. I still wanted to do one more take for insurance. On the second ad-libbed take, the dialogue was similar but different, with almost identical length, which says something about the human, inner clock mechanisms. That did it; I'd now have to wait for the film to come back, synched with sound to determine if I was successful. I conclude that if I don't have it in either of the two takes, I was going to find a real actor.

This now left enough film to shoot scene 97, Rick on the phone, in the office, talking to a customer. The scene concluded the shoot for the weekend. Tomorrow, though, would be a rare weeknight shoot with a borrowed limousine for scenes 28, 29, and 30.

16

Bjs, Limos, And Cops

Monday, December 8

I had arranged the use of a gratis limo from Moonlight Limo Rentals weeks earlier. They told me a Monday night would be perfect because they had practically no business on that night. The scene was intended to be placed on an interstate, which would have made shooting very difficult. My scouting a location led me across the street from the Moonlight Limo Service. It is the very long driveway to my town's middle school. Lined with streetlights, it afforded me the opportunity to shoot the establishing shot of the limo cruising down the interstate, while having the privacy to shoot the outdoor racy scenes without passersby.

The establishing shots were pretty uneventful.

The limo interior shots were tough because my lens, at its widest focal length, was just able to get the scene composed. The lighting was challenge number two. I purchased a video light for my camcorder and used it for the illumination of the scene. I was just barely able to get the exposure up to the maximum aperture of f/2.8 of my film camera. The camcorder and light were actually positioned closer to the subject in my film camera to achieve this lighting juggling act.

I had cast TJ Curran and Jeannie Sullivan for this particular scene in the limo. I called them both and gave them directions to the school. I inadvertently gave TJ a wrong turn on the way to the schoolyard. Consequently, he drove around Newport for over a half hour trying to locate us. A tense half-hour as I bided time preparing for the shoot, talking to Jeannie Sullivan and the limo driver, Bill Hetland. I had asked several friends to come with their cars, as I needed background action.

The plan was to have the cars approach the rear of the limo when it was parked at the side of the road. As they arrived at the end of the driveway, they would turn to the left in a U-turn and head back to the starting point, several hundred feet, only to do another U-turn. The net effect on the scene was that it appeared to be a busy interstate with steady streams of cars going both ways.

The intent was for them to witness the event outside the limo within the illumination of the headlights. As we shot the limo driver pulling up the pants of the Pete character, a Middletown police cruiser pulled into the schoolyard driveway to check on the goings-on. The limo driver walked up to the squad car and carried a conversation with the patrolman. I was sweating that the cop was going to send us on our way, and I'd be faced with a partial shoot that I'd have to match elsewhere. Not a good option. In the meantime, I was thinking it was too bad I couldn't use the cruiser in the scene to heighten the situation. The addition of the cruiser pulling up behind the limo as the driver is pulling up Pete's pants and underwear would be priceless but given the reality… forget about it. Back to reality Bill Hetland, the limo driver, said goodbye to the patrolman. As the cop car left, Bill told me the patrolman was a friend of his and he asked us to get the shoot over with and move on as he wasn't sure of the legality.

"Friend, friend?" I asked. "Could you call him back?"

I told Bill of my idea of the cop car and he thought it was great, except he'd have to call the station to have that particular officer paged, which would raise some curiosity we didn't need to raise. Another lost opportunity to increase production value. It definitely would have made the scene funnier. Well, no crying over spilt milk.

Heeding the police warning, we resumed shooting the scene outside the limo while the driver pulled up Pete's pants and underwear. The procession of cars resumed their movements, and everyone was laughing. Whether they were in cars or on the crew. A few takes and we were done for a week and a half due to actors' availability and scheduling issues. A needed breather as we entered the tail end of production. This would be my Christmas shopping break.

17

My Movie Comes To Life As Titanic Sails Into History

Friday, December 19

I'd taken the day off from my job for two events. The first event was spending a whole day with my editor Tom Ohanian. Up until now, he'd shown me segments of scenes pieced together that almost had the effects of seeing a magic trick. This time, I'd been shooting pieces of scenes for six months and seeing them strung together in a cohesive manner…a sight to behold. That day, we were going to connect some of the scenes together into a linear series.

The second event was the opening of the much awaited and hyped movie *TITANIC*. Coinciding with this was the opening of the Stadium seating Dolby Digital theater in our area. The first one of its kind. I'd usually traveled over an hour to attend a quality theater presentation and now we had one nearby. I went to the theater early in the morning to advance purchase eight tickets for the evening performance. My friends and family were to meet there after I'd finished editing.

I marveled at the cinema palace and was anxious to see *Titanic* there. The fact that Tom co-invented the Avid system, which was used to edit *Titanic,* and was involved as a technical advisor, and would now be editing my movie was a thrill too much to describe.

I arrived at Tom's home and he was ready with the Avid system warmed up and ready to go. He scanned several scenes that he'd already assembled, as he determined which ones were to be put together linearly. As he worked, I marveled at the technology and art merging. Tom would take two successive scenes, put them together, and play them a few times to evaluate flow. It was interesting to see that sometimes it worked as planned, and other times it didn't feel right.

When it doesn't, you need to evaluate both scenes and determine if they need changes as to when they end and where the succeeding scene begins. That's the magic of the Avid nonlinear system. You can alter any scenes in any way and then A-B them to death. The creative possibilities are infinite. I'd never edited conventionally but I couldn't imagine ever wanting to do it the old way once this system is tried. You could never explore the possibilities that are available without this approach. I thank God for Tom Ohanian and the Avid System that he co-invented. Watching him manipulate the pacing of the scenes by when you come in and when you get out is a revelation. This is also where a new filmmaker like myself learns how much extra footage is necessary to shoot at the head and tail of the scene. The flipside is you could try to be stingy, shoot tight, and reduce the options available to the editor. Not a good situation. When you look at the ultimate objective, which is to make the best film you can, it's not worth economizing.

We wrapped our full day of editing at about 6 p.m.. I left Tom's with an incredible sense of accomplishment and self-worth. I was making a movie, and it looked like one. This was unbelievable. I drove over to the multiplex to find my friends and family arriving at the same time. I'd always been one to travel to a good multiplex 60 miles way to see a movie, but most of my party hadn't experienced a high-quality theater. *Titanic* was definitely the movie to see under these circumstances. We were awed by the experience of sights and sound. I was still on a high from my editing experience. That day went down as one of the best total days of my life.

Saturday, December 20

We were back at Tom and Steve Scott's Red Farm Studio for a morning of shooting the Turkey stuffing display scenes. The corrugated display was designed by Steve Longa and Jeremy Hood, the designers for the box company I work for in real life. I asked them to design two displays. One display that was correctly designed and one that was unstable. The correct one was used when Rick is showing it to his plant manager. The unstable one was the one that is delivered to the angry customer. Steve Scott is the non-speaking manager, and Don Cornell is the purchasing manager who was there when the defective order arrived. All three men in the scene brought a change of clothing to film the two scenes, which took place on two different days in the film. The first in which Rick takes the order for the display and the second scene was when the customer received the order and, due to a miscommunication, got a display that wouldn't stand up.

We had to get over the laughing fits during the rehearsal and had to dry run it with cast composed before I'd roll film on the actual take—always a concern when filming a scene that's very funny.

The actors really earned their salt under the circumstances. After completing the two scenes in

Steve and Tom's father's office, we moved the equipment downstairs to Steve's office, which had a totally different look, for the scene where the obnoxious, laughing purchasing agent tests Rick's patience. The scene was written about and to include a guy I knew that laughs hysterically after every sentence he spoke. An odd trait that always got a reaction from any observer. Well, I asked the real laughing man to play the role and he gladly accepted. Only problem was, as we got close to the shooting date, his wife decided he didn't need to display his idiosyncratic laugh in a movie. I related my most recent dilemma to Ace who, once again, pulled a rabbit out of the hat. He knew a fellow stand-up comic whose sketch is to laugh at everything. It sounded too good to be true. I asked him to contact his friend and see if he'd be interested. The answer to both questions was yes.

He arrived right on time, with the prepared reading, laugh track included. We dry ran the scene and he was every bit as quirky as my originally planned actor. I was feeling like the most blessed individual. Things go wrong, but they almost always right themselves. It turned out to be another hard to contain yourself as you're filming kind of scene.

After we completed that scene, we adjourned to the parking lot where we shot the scene where Rick takes the display out of the car when he arrives at the Turkey Stuffing Company. That completed, we headed back to Crystal Thermoplastics Studio for a quick two scenes in the hallway where Rick is going to and from his office to Edward Cox's. A change of clothes was the only variable. The only scenes remaining would be done on our way home.

When I rewrote the end of the picture, I added a scene where we showed what everyone was doing 'now'. Bonnie's character is happily married to someone else and she now has a baby. In real life Terri, (Bonnie) did have her baby in November and her shooting days were behind her. I thought this would be a great time to shoot her real husband and baby now during the holidays with their Christmas tree in the background. The scene is M.O.S. with Rick's retrospective voice at the end of the film. We hadn't seen Terri or her husband in months, so it was a fun get together. Fun, but awkward, because I brought up the fact that we needed to shoot one other new scene as a bridge to tie together the other scenes in the movie. The scene is where Rick tells Bonnie he has a thing for her and plants his first kiss on her. It was kind of awkward to shoot this scene in Terri's kitchen, while her husband took care of the baby in the other room. Her husband was a real trooper as he cared for his newborn while hearing and imagining Rick's love proclamation and subsequent lip lock on his wife.

This is just one more example of the things you do and get involved in when making a film. With these two scenes completed, we were so close to the end of production, I could taste it.

Sunday, December 21

Rick is in the barber shop scene at the end of the movie. I scouted the greater Providence area for a very typical barbershop to film this M.O.S. scene. The shop owner and his son-in-law were both interested in being in the picture, so I used this opportunity to place my nephew Dave, the soundman, in this scene as an extra. The scene's intent was to continue the running gag where Rick is once more ushering the character Dave around town on his personal errands, which now happens to be at a barber shop. Ace adlibs once again as he interacts with the audience, breaking the fourth wall again. He looks to the audience and shakes his head as if to say, nothing has changed. A quick roll of the camera and we were off to Warwick, Rhode Island, to film the Bob Wish and Rick talking in the car scene. This scene exists for expository reasons. Their dialogue is to explain who they are as people, and how and why they got to this place and time in their lives.

Bob learns why Rick took this job, and Rick learns a bit of the life of his new mentor, who is a little lonely. Bob credits his relationship with his customers to fulfill some of the emptiness. The scenes were filmed rather smoothly, with just enough sentiment expressed to understand our two heroes. We wrapped this expository scene and went to lunch.

I bought lunch for the cast and crew to celebrate our wrapping this dry but necessary scene. We all knew what remained to be shot that day; no one was excited.

18

Ten Degree Beach Day

The time had come…the dreaded beach scene.

When I rewrote the end of the movie at the request of the editor, Tom Ohanian, one of the new montages included Bob Wish on a beach. The voiceover explains that he's kicking back in the Caribbean. Having no budget and living in the Ocean State, there wasn't a decision to make. I drove around the state looking for a beach that had a steep enough incline, in a short enough distance, so that my camera only picked up beach and not any buildings or scenery that would give the location away. This criterion was met on Oakland Beach in Warwick, Rhode Island. You would think that that criteria, in a state with 400 miles of shoreline, would be easy to find, but not so. I'm sure there was a better choice, but I wasn't up to endlessly searching for it. Oakland Beach would have to do.

The scene was shot M.O.S., so all John Cicero (Bob Wish) had to do was sit in a lounge chair at the water's edge, talking on a cell phone, wearing a T-shirt in 10° weather. Fortunately, it was a sunny day with no wind, so it wasn't completely uncomfortable. Of course, the crew were in winter coats while Bob was in a bathing suit. A tip from Tom Ohanian was to have Bob put ice cubes in his mouth to prevent his breath from showing in the cold air as he spoke. Bob was really happy about this. Sitting on a beach in 10° weather in shorts and T-shirt sucking on an ice cube while pretending he's in the Caribbean. Now that's acting. What made the whole scenario worse was that the crew were dressed in long winter coats with layers underneath. Even in the face of guilt, no one took the sympathetic measure to remove their coats in name of political correctness.

Because this scene was shot M.O.S., John Cicero was saying into the phone, "I can't believe these assholes have me on a fucking beach in winter, making like I'm enjoying myself." Another memorable, moviemaking moment. We quickly shot this scene, bade goodbye to John, celebrating the end of shooting with him, packed up, and headed to Newport to shoot the scene with Rick and his grandmother.

This scene dovetailed the new scene that was written that raises the tension levels between Rick and his boss and demonstrated his devotion to his grandmother. The shoot took place in Ethel Groff's (grandmother) actual home. Ethel's living room had such a homey look that it could have been a sitting room at a nursing home. It would work. I gave the new script pages to Ethel the week before. My appeasement to her was that this would be our last shoot. Honestly, déjà vu—I'd told her that before.

The shoot went quickly and painlessly. There was one more location after that. Again, we were shooting a newly written scene for the revised ending. The scene depicted Rick several years after the tale, with explaining voiceover. He's at home with his boss's daughter, now his wife, and his young child. When casting his wife, Ace made the totally realistic suggestion that we ask the Farrellys if we could borrow Cameron Diaz as his wife for this scene.

"She may still be in town filming *There's Something About Mary,*" he thinks.

I think this long shooting schedule had affected his prefrontal cortex. I assured him I had it already covered, I had casted a perfect wife for him. The house we used was my cousin Duke Jr.'s new home. The voice over explained that Rick had a family now. At the time, Duke Jr. had three young children and I intended to shoot this scene depicting Rick hugging his wife on the sofa with a camera move down to show his young family on the floor playing. Well, the three kids were not what you'd call cooperative. Rehearsals went terribly so there was no point rolling film for this futile exercise.

We removed the two older kids and stuck with the youngest son, Jonathan. My ultimate intent was for Jonathan to do on screen what he did, and he did. I thank God that the take ended the way it did, where Jonathan is in the box looking around, then rests his chin on the box edge and looks at the camera which ends the voiceover and the movie. Perfect, and it happened on a wing and a prayer. It had taken a few takes but we knew we were done when it happened.

As difficult as the shoot went, deep down I knew all would be right because of an omen-like event that touched us on Friday night only two days prior. I had cast an actress, Erin Casey, as Rick's wife. I had auditioned Erin eight months earlier for the Bonnie character. I had decided to cast Terri Leander instead for reasons I could justify at the time. This choice had caused me to always regret not having a role for Erin. Erin is an absolutely beautiful woman.

When I rewrote the ending and needed Rick's wife, the choice was narrowed to one. I called Erin and she was interested. I told Ace of my choice and he was just dying to see who this stunning Erin Casey is. Ace kept asking me, are you sure she's right? Is she really that beautiful, sure we can't get Cameron Diaz? Yes, yes, and no again, Ace, trust me.

Back to the Friday night I'm describing. Ace had moved away from Rhode Island but returned to R.I. to shoot the movie during the day and visit his old haunts and friends on weekend nights. Ace had visited a bar that Friday night where he expected to run into old friends. He did. He saw an old acquaintance that he hadn't seen in years. The old, "what have you been you up to," talk ensues, and Ace informed his friend that he'd been filming a movie for the past six months. His friend informed him that his girlfriend, who was somewhere in the bar, was also in a movie, filming a scene that very Sunday. Just then, a beautiful woman came out of the crowd and her boyfriend made the introduction, "Ace meet my girlfriend, Erin Casey." Ace just about fell over.

He shook her hand and said, "You're playing someone's wife in a movie on Sunday?"

She reeled surprisingly and wondered how he knew.

Ace followed up with, "I'm the guy you're married to."

I would love to know how you would go

about coming up with the mathematical probability of this happening. When Ace related the story to me on Saturday morning when we shot the turkey stuffing scene, I was equally as shocked. I am not superstitious, but I couldn't help but see this as some sort of sign or good omen. When you're working on a high-stakes project, you look for any symbol or sign that you're on the right track. I couldn't think of any sign more significant than something that was as against all odds as this. My choice was dead on, as Erin was the perfect dream woman and her screen actions accomplished what was needed. The shoot was perfect in every respect. I was high as a kite after that shoot. Another weekend of shooting concluded on a high note.

Saturday, December 27

There was only one scene to shoot that day with only Ace and Elliott needed. Back to the Packet Bldg. to shoot the scene where Edward Cox threatens Rick that his job is in jeopardy. This is the scene that will precede the Rick visits grandmother scene we shot last weekend. Elliott as Edward Cox was just great delivering the lines that build the tension and gets the audience in Rick's corner. Elliott delivered as the dick-headed boss everyone loves to hate.

19

Theater Reshoot And Clean Up

We were reshooting the movie theater scene that I blew due to my inexperience a month prior. The shoot was planned for late morning, and I reassembled all my friends who were there on November 9, the day of the original shoot. To fill in my earlier morning, I asked my girlfriend Carol Kent to be the leg lady as a backup to the original leg lady. Just a neurotic second guessing on my part. As I looked at the end of the film, my insecurities flared up in the unlikeliest manifestations. The insurance leg shot took place on my street and was composed in such a way that it could be edited in if needed. A quick M.O.S. scene and we packed up for our reshoot of the movie theater scene. Unfortunately, several of my friends and acquaintances were unable to make the shoot, yet new ones were able to.

I actually felt bad that people got left on the cutting room floor because of my inexperience. One good thing that came out of the reshoot was that my friend Patty Sylvia could come as an extra with her sister who died unexpectedly two years later, so we have her in a few of the background shots. This shoot resulted in the look I needed. I changed the lighting and film stock and felt I got it right this time.

Thanks again to all the extras for showing up and for Joe Jarvis, the owner of Jane Pickens Theater, for not only exhibiting independent cinema, but supporting it by allowing me to shoot twice in his theater.

January 1

This tale of the shoot could not be complete without one more ongoing gag which turned out to be more fix-it stuff. I once again needed to call Ethel Groff in front of the camera in spite of my telling her we were done with her several times before. When Tom and I edited her scene in the beginning of the film at the college graduation cocktail reception, she turns to her grandson to ask, "Where is your girlfriend?"

Well, the best take of that scene just happened

to be the last take on that roll, the one where the roll of film ran out before Ethel turned her head. Without Ethel turning her head there lacked the transitional footage to make it a smooth cut to close-up which was to follow. So, I just needed a close-up of Ethel turning her head. It also needed to be at a location similar to the garden party shot in September. I also failed to mention that the opening garden party dialogue was too ponderous and static, so Tom and I decided it needed a rewrite and a reshoot. Sorry Ethel.

To complicate matters, it was January in the Northeast and it was very cold. Freezing to be exact. I needed to stage the dialogue indoors and have it cut into the garden party footage that already existed. I rewrote it to take place in the Great Hall at Ochre Court at Salve Regina College in Newport, Rhode Island. This is the same building used for the mansion in the opening scenes of Jim Cameron's *True Lies,* which was shot there in the winter of 1994. So, there I was, three years later, shooting my movie with Ethel Groff in the same location. I don't know for sure, but would this be defined or considered as Karma?

The new scene was better all-around partly because of dialogue improvement, but also for intimacy and grandeur. I loved the new feeling in the scene where you experienced the magnificence of the ballroom. It also became a much more intimate introduction of our protagonist and his grandmother. I was saved again by a fortuitous problem in the originally shot scene that led me to rewrite and re-shoot for a much better result. An added bonus to the scene is that the line, "It just took me ten years," which was intended as an exposition, turned out to be a laugher. Audiences crack up on that line. I just didn't conceive or intend for it to be that way, but hey, I'll take a bow for it now.

After shooting the indoor scene, we bundled Ethel up and went outside to shoot the filler scene where she turns her head M.O.S.. She'd done her hair and dressed the same as that September day. I set her up with greenery behind her head to make the setting as nondescript as possible. Hopefully, nondescript would edit in without being obvious. I then angled in Ethel in relationship to the sun to duplicate the relative angle of the original shoot. Someone off-camera would peel Ethel's overcoat off, we'd shoot the scene, call cut, then throw her coat back on her. I also asked her not to breathe during the take, so that her breath wouldn't be visible in the cold air. Ethel was terrific considering all we'd put this woman through. A couple takes of this and we'd be back inside to get pickup shots of Rick in reverse angle of when he's talking with his grandmother.

You're obviously wondering why we didn't

get it earlier, when we were set up for the scene? It was because the outdoor pickup scene with Ethel needed to be in sunlight to match the scene shot in September. The day was overcast, and the sun popped out during the indoor scene so we re-prioritized and broke off to get it. Flexibility is a must in filmmaking. It can't be repeated enough. This done, we tore down and drove up to Providence to get the pick-up shots of Rick and Lester conversing in the car. We found a vacant parking lot on the waterfront to get it. When I called, "CUT" on this scene, the production phase was officially over.

There is a strange feeling that comes over you when you reach the end of something. It's a bittersweet combination of elation that it is over and sorrow that something fun and sometimes aggravating is coming to an end. I wasn't feeling all that bad though, because I recognized that in filmmaking, it's not really over until the film is in a theater being unspooled in a projector.

20

Four Months Of Editing

During the shooting of the film Tom Ohanian, the editor, was receiving my Beta and DAT tapes, merging the two, and assembling the takes that were the best. Because we were stingy in shooting, Tom did not have a lot of material to work with. It was probably for the best because Tom was working on projects on the left coast, so he was commuting back and forth, juggling jobs. It was all coming together very nicely though.

Having completed all photography, I met with Tom on a regular basis. Tom had edited all the easy scenes that didn't need interpretation and saved the ones that needed discussion for when I was available. You can't imagine what it's like to watch two or more similar scenes repeatedly, attempting to either pick a favorite or find a difference between the two. Sometimes easy and most of the time the nuances are so slight that you obsessively watch with the goal of picking a favorite only to second guess your own gut feeling. Maddening at times. A movie editor really earns his or her money. Your attention span and concentration are taxed to the max. This process took four months and in that time span, I probably had seen my movie accumulatively 20 times. It's no wonder I've heard filmmakers say they never watch their own movies. They burned it all up at the front end.

As we approached the mid-point in the process, Tom thought it would be a good idea to get some press. He contacted Michael Janusonis, the movie critic of the Providence Journal, to do an interview. The date was set, and I was a nervous wreck. I had grown up reading his movie reviews and felt he was a pretty tough critic. He gets paid to say what he thinks. All I'm picturing is him watching portions of my little film and then picking it apart. OOUUCCHH!

The day finally arrived, and we met at Tom's. Michael was very polite and genuinely interested in my story as he asked me about the film and what drove me to do it. Not a monster at all. When the chatting ended, he asked if he could see some scenes. Tom had already prepped the scenes in advance and fired up the computer monitor with the first scene, the one we filmed at the Jane Pickens Theater. The scene just showed the audience watching the movie screen with only the back wall visible behind them.

Michael exclaimed, "You shot this in Jane Pickens!"

Only a movie critic would recognize the back wall of a theater, an indication of one spending too much time in movie theaters. He watched the scene and laughed when he was supposed to. Wow, that was good. Tom queues up another funny scene, and Michael laughs again on cue. Is this really happening? A few more scenes, and more laughter at the right times again. I was so damned excited.

Michael wound down the interview, stating he had all he needed, and bade us goodbye.

Tom and I were high fiving. A week later, the article was in the Providence Journal, accompanied by the photo their staff photographer took of me with a James Bond theater stand up Tom had as a souvenir from working on that film.

Well, this is what people refer to as their 15 minutes of fame. The flood gates opened. My telephone started ringing and continued through the day. The first call was from WPRO FM station asking to interview me on the air. It was now 6 a.m. and I was barely awake. I didn't trust my ability to carry an intelligent conversation within earshot of the entire Rhode Island market ten minutes after awakening, so I asked them if we could do it another time? They said yes, call us tomorrow at 8 a.m.. I did just that the next morning and they told me they couldn't do the interview because they had the "Psychic reader scheduled." We never did do the interview, which says a lot about yesterday's news and the perishability of the 15 minutes of fame.

21

A Composer That Gets It

Coinciding with my shooting and Tom's editing was the then unavoidable hiring or recruiting of a composer for the musical score. Considering I had no budget for music, I decided to contact music schools to attempt to recruit a composer. I went to both the New England Conservatory of Music and the Berklee College of Music, both in Boston, and put up a sheet on their bulletin boards inviting students to audition for a no pay movie project. I stated that if my film was successfully sold, they would be paid for their contribution. I had no idea how this would be received.

Within one week, replies were arriving in my mailbox. In short order, I had received eighteen replies including a professor from the famous Julliard School in New York. He was teaming with a friend from the Berklee College of Music. To say I felt privileged is an understatement. Prior to putting up the notices, I decided that I needed a fair method of evaluating any respondents, if I was lucky enough to receive any. I had Tom create a five-minute video cassette of montages of scenes that had either emotional weight or comedy. A five-minute litmus test, if you will. My thought was that if the respondent could do these five minutes to my satisfaction, they could do the whole thing.

I contacted Tom and excitedly told him that I needed eighteen copies of this prospective cassette. When I picked up the cassettes, Tom was finishing up the edit on another film entitled *Code of Ethics*. I watched as scenes transitioned on his screen and was struck by how good the soundtrack sounded…truly professional. I asked Tom who wrote the music.

He answered, "A composer from Wakefield, R.I. named Grant Maloy Smith." A local, I observed.

I asked Tom, "I assume he gets paid?"

"Yes," responds Tom.

"Damn," retorted I.

I took my eighteen cassettes and headed home where eighteen boxes and letters of instruction awaited these cassettes to be mailed. Within days of mailing, phone calls with questions started coming in. I was happy to hear that some of the respondents were putting thought into my project. This was just too exciting.

I must mention now that I am non-musical. I mean, I love music, but I do not read it, play it, or even understand how anyone goes about writing it. It is truly a mystery to me, yet here I was about to pass judgement on people who do. Then the earliest video cassettes with music dubbed on them started arriving. I set quiet time aside to watch any cassette and really tried to absorb how different musicians interpreted these scenes.

The first one did not grab me. *Oh well,* I thought, *I guess he just didn't get it.* Second one, same result. I took a day off, then watched the third, same result.

Uh-oh, do I know what I'm doing or am I just fussy? Then the phone call came.

"Hi, this is Grant Smith."

I gathered my thoughts, realized who it was, and replied, "I love what you did on *Code of Ethics*."

Grant thanked me and told me why he called. He had been with Tom recently and Tom showed him some footage of my film. Tom spoke very well of my project, and Grant liked what he saw. Grant decided he wanted to be involved. I was flattered but also concerned about the money thing. I told him of my non-existent budget and how I was personally funding this dream. He told me he would like to read my script and decide what he could offer. I sent him a copy, and he liked it enough to offer a back end deal where I would pay him when and if the film sells.

I was blown away. Here was someone I didn't know, but whose work I respected, and he believed in my project as I did. How could you not feel a kinship with someone that offered a sacrifice of this magnitude? I loved this guy, but could he please me?

Grant came to my home with his youngest son, Alec, to pick up his prospective five-minute video cassette. I liked him immediately. He displayed a good sense of humor, so we really connected. He asked me my musical influences and who I'd been listening to recently.

Funny, no one else had asked me those questions. I wished him good luck as he left with his homework assignment.

Over the next month, more video cassettes continued to arrive at my home. It was getting ridiculous; I didn't like any of them. I was seriously questioning my sanity. Maybe I really didn't know what I was doing. Is it possible I could get this far in the filmmaking process and fall short at the finish line? I was stressing as I realized that almost all eighteen cassettes were back, and I was not happy. Grant hadn't called me back yet either, so I gave him a call and he told me he was still working on it. No time commitment referenced or false hope I could hang my hat on. I'm an impatient guy, but I didn't want Grant to know this.

I politely thanked him, hung up, and stressed like cornered prey. I let Tom know that at that point in time, Grant Smith was my Hail Mary. I felt the discomfort of being very vulnerable with nowhere else to turn. I waited a few weeks and called Grant again. He was almost done and would mail it out soon.

It arrived. I felt as if the cassette in my hands was a life jacket and my boat was sinking.

I popped it in, took a deep breath, watched, and listened. What I saw and heard was very natural. Seamless. Like all the movies I'd watched in my life, the music matched the scene, and you didn't get a sensation of second guessing the score. It just was, and this is what I was experiencing as I joyfully watched the five minutes of musical synergy.

To say I was out of my mind with happiness is far from exaggeration. I called Grant and told him the job was his and that I couldn't wait to see the results for the whole film. Grant told me to send him a Betamax copy of the cassette, with time codes imprinted, once the film was locked.

Locked is the industry term for when all editorial decisions are made, implemented, and completed, with no other changes to be made. Grant could then custom write the music that precisely fit the scenes with pinpoint accuracy.

22

Post Master Sound

Post sound is the stage of a film where sound needs to be created to either augment what's there or repair what needs fixing. Tom Ohanian had introduced me to three guys who run a company named Post Master Sound, a catchy double entendre. They, like Tom, are also employees of Avid Corp. by day and moonlight in a film-related business by night. I am appreciative that I could make these industry connections with a one-stop shopping experience.

They watched my finished video cassette and made a laundry list of the fixes that were required. I asked them to seed them in order of must be fixed, should be fixed, and would be nice to fix. This would allow me to budget how much money I wanted to throw in this direction.

The list caused some serious talks with myself. It would be nice to address all the fixes, but not financially prudent, given I was paying all the bills. I determined the most important fixes were dialogue related. Unintelligible dialogue is a high priority, and I had several scenes that needed "looping" or ADR (automated dialogue replacement). The process involves going into a soundproof studio where a monitor plays the scene which needs looping and the actor or actors voice their lines in synch with their lips on screen. It may sound easy, but it isn't because the proper delivery and emotion must be present for it to play well. I basically had to direct the performance to match the already locked movie image. We would discuss the scene, watch the scene, and then record the new audio in sync with the scene. The actor would strive to lip sync to their image on the monitor. Many takes later, we got them all done. The sound guys would then replace the faulty sound with the new sound only after they would sculpt and add the ambient sounds that would match what existed in the scene. Pretty amazing stuff. Once Post Master Sound finished their end of the film, I met with them one last time to create the closing credits. I dictated, and they typed the information into what is now the closing credits. They sent all this and the newly created sound tapes to Tom Ohanian who married up all these elements for the finished product. The movie *BOXedMAN* was now complete.

Now that Tom and I finally locked the picture, I drove the Beta tape to Grant's home that same day as though it would save some time. Do I sound anxious? For me, the waiting had begun.

In a couple of months, Grant delivered his totally scored movie to me. I set aside a two hour, totally alert time of day to watch the movie in its entirety. I was prepared to be as honest as I could with myself and dislike anything that did not feel or sound right. Was I ever surprised. There was nothing that jumped out at me, and I was looking.

Grant did it! Nailed it totally. I was now in possession of a totally and completely finished film! Mission Accomplished. Words cannot capture the emotion of what this feels like. I was now ready to share it with audiences.

23

Film Festival Debut

The final product was finished, and it was time to show it off. The obvious place to submit it to was film festivals, of which there are countless. I subscribed to too many film magazines just for the addresses and dates. You cannot possibly comprehend the individual requirements of submission.

First of all, they all required a fee, which is the only constant. There are forms to fill out, with different requirements for each fest. None of the forms are alike. Some of the requirements ask for publicity photos and differing numbers of them from fest to fest. Some had conditions of when the film was finished. Some asked for cast lists with photos. They all had conditions and hoops to jump through so you couldn't create a one form fits all submission process. They all had wording that had you putting on your lawyer hat and combing for details that could be overlooked. You wouldn't want to be rejected or not considered because you missed crossing a T.

My biggest problem was that I did not have a film print available for submission. A film print is created by having all my film clips cut and spliced back together to match the Avid digital edit that Tom Ohanian created in his computer. The key codes that are part of the video daily's match up to the actual film frames. It is just a matter of assembling to match the video edit. Then this finished, spliced-together, 16mm film is sent to a lab to create a 35mm copy, which is what is required for showing in theaters and festivals. We're talking about, at the time, a cost of close to $100,000. This figure was definitely not in my budget. My strategy was to explain my predicament in my film festival applications and ask if they would accept a Beta Video copy for exhibition. I would possibly sell my soul and make a 35mm print if I was accepted by a high-profile festival such as Sundance in Utah or Cannes in France, which was not to be. I did get rejection letters from them both. I can actually say I had something to be rejected for from these two iconic festivals. Not everyone can say that, so I do have that going for me.

I did get accepted by festivals in Lisbon, Portugal and Athens, Greece. They both explained that they would put me up in hotels and I only needed to send them my 35mm prior to the festival. They both clearly did not read my application with the same care with which I read theirs. I wrote back to both, asking the Beta Video question again and got no response. This whole exercise was feeling like Nick Pasyanos was funding film festivals all over the world with no personal benefit to himself. I was sending out thousands of dollars in fees and piling up rejection letters as a totally lopsided trade. SXSW Festival in Austin, TX sent me a rejection letter, but included an invitation to a seminar on how to get exposure for your film.

Did I just enter the Twilight Zone? Wouldn't I have gotten exposure for my film if they had accepted it? I sometimes think I was put on this earth to live by irony. There was one festival that did send me an acceptance, and it was nearby, The Rhode Island International Film Festival. I got an acceptance letter from them and was thrilled but not surprised. After all, I am a local and with all the local publicity, how could they snub me? It just so happened that Bobby Farrelly of the Farrelly Brothers was the chairperson. Their new film, *There's Something About Mary* was about to be released on July 15th, three weeks before

BOXedMAN was to be shown for the first time at the festival.

Carol and I went to see *There's Something About Mary* on opening night. The movie was as funny as could be, and there was an incredible surprise that made the night for me. Within the context of the movie, I counted 14 scenes that had similarities to my movie.

As we watched, the common threads of *BOXedMAN* and *Mary* kept jumping off the screen, either thematically or in identical dialogue. There were so many that Carol and I kept looking at each other eerily as they appeared.

The first one came ten minutes into the movie when the protagonist Ted shows up at Mary's house and is greeted by her African American stepfather, who proceeds to give Ted a hard time. A ball busting hard time. (My film has the protagonist, Rick, getting the same treatment by an African American business owner.)

Mary's father's opening line is, "What the hell do you want?" and Rick is greeted by the proudly Italian American purchasing agent whose line is, "What the fuck do you want?"

Two rapid fire coincidences. Ted then enters the house where he witnesses his date Mary descending the stairs. Their eyes lock on each other as the scene unfolds in slow-mo. (Just how my meeting scene of Rick and Bonnie exists, eyes locked, filmed in slow-mo.)

Moments after that scene, a photo on a wall is shown of the stepfather sporting a 60's era Afro. That was a scene I envisioned for my Black business owners wall (as his business was in Black hair care products), but jettisoned it as I didn't have the time, resources, and all that was necessary to buy a wig and add that to the scene. It did make me wish I had had made the extra effort though. It was a funny touch that would have very appropriately juiced up my scene. Another interesting interconnection.

The next coincidental scene is when Ted and Dom are sitting in a bar, elbows touching, in a two shot (two people in one shot), talking about his love interest. The camera angle would be the bartender's perspective. *BOXedMAN* has the identical framing, the same relational characters, talking the same subject.

Next Ted becomes inadvertently mixed in with a group of gay guys. He attempts to distance himself from the group. Rick, in *BOXedMAN,* becomes self-consciously uncomfortable that he is mistakenly viewed as being gay because of his best friend's action in a movie theater.

There's a scene in both films of a guy by the roadside with his pants down around his ankles.

There's a scene in both films of a guy getting a blowjob, with identical camera angles.

Both films have a character that drives a shit box car that runs on after the car is turned off.

Both films also have an antagonist that is a pizza delivery guy.

In *Mary,* Ted masturbates before his date with Mary (the infamous hair gel scene).

In *BOXedMAN,* Rick tells Bonnie he just went in the men's room to masturbate because she temptingly turned him on in the office.

Both films have a funny person with a sexual obsession.

The remaining coincidences were cases of identical dialogue. The protagonists using the term "sick fuck," and calling someone, "a piece of shit," were identical terms used in both movies.

Very strange, curious, yet affirming that my writing had something in common to the Farrellys. Was this Karma? Was this an omen? How could I not think this?

I left the theater in a state of intense excitement. Having 11 scenes with similarities to this juggernaut of a film made me feel like I was on the right track. I'll go with omen.

This thought or delusion, however you interpret it, would sustain me as I awaited the Film Festival debut date. My next omen moment was the morning of the opening of the festival.

I was out working my sales job and stopped for a bite to eat in Providence, approximately 20 miles from Woonsocket, which is where the festival was held. Outside the hot dog joint on Hope Street, who do I run into but Bobby Farrelly, who had the same craving as I. We made casual conversation about the festival and his role as chairperson of the festival. He wished me luck, and I pocketed another omen because...what are the odds?

Later that afternoon I attended the opening ceremony confident that this was going to be a heady experience. It was terrific to meet other film makers and feel a part of a fraternity of artists you've always admired. We talked about our films and committed to see each other's.

Two days later my film was shown to a full house. In attendance were several actors who starred in the production, other filmmakers, and a lot of curious people who had been reading the press for my film. What a bizarre experience. To see your personal creation in a darkened theater with a crowd of people is strange indeed. To hear communal laughter, on cue, at all the right places, is an experience that is surrealistic.

At the end of the film, the memory of the applause is something I will never forget. The expression of congratulations from the viewers in the lobby only added to the craziness of it all. In the fray of people in the lobby was the film crew from the Providence ABC affiliate, who interviewed me for the evening news. We finished the interview, said our good-byes, and headed home. The biggest surprise was still in store.

I got home, listened to my answering machine, and almost dropped to the floor. Bobby Farrelly called to say he missed my viewing but heard so much about it that he wanted to see a copy. Here was a guy who had the biggest film of the summer, breaking records in theaters nationwide, and he was asking to see my film because he heard how funny it was? I felt euphoric and became so distracted that I completely forgot to watch and record my interview on the nightly news. It didn't even occur to me until the next day. I wasn't all that saddened because I busied myself packaging up the movie copy to mail to Bobby. That same day I was invited to an open forum where I sat with a panel of filmmakers for a question-and-answer session from the film festival attendees. It was very strange indeed—me, as an expert, on a panel with other filmmakers answering questions from a couple hundred attendees. There were repeated questions about my movie, from the other filmmakers and attendees regarding the similarities to the Farrelly's new film. The similarities I saw just weren't in my mind. Others picked up on it and asked if we collaborated or hung out together. The answer was no to both questions, I just credited it to the fact that we were both from Rhode Island, so it must be a Rhode Island thing. The week just kept getting weirder.

Due to the positive first screening, the festival director set up a second screening at the Brown University theater, which was a sellout. The audience laughed at all the right places, confirming that the first successful viewing was not a fluke. Holy crap, this is really happening, it's not a dream!

The Festival concluded with a closing ceremony with the announcement that *BOXedMAN* earned and was awarded the Best of Fest Audience Award. This award is determined by attendees voting their favorite film, rather than the festival committee. The surprises kept on coming, but eventually any run must come to an end. My high would carry for a period of time but eventually would be replaced with the disappointment of those damn film festival rejection letters that were clogging my mailbox. I had now reached the turning point. Here's where all the elation and emotional highs of a successful film completion reach the turning point with an opposite trajectory.

Bobby Farrelly left me another voicemail a week later to tell me he watched my movie. He raved about how funny it was and how much he enjoyed it. He said that I was all set, and that he would like to hold on to it for a while to show his brother, who was out of town. The message was 123 seconds long, I know, because I listened to it repeatedly. I couldn't believe his response. They presently had the biggest box office hit of the summer and he said my film was funny. I was probably the happiest and most excited I could ever be. That is until I hit the wall.

Weeks later, I received my cassette back from Bobby, with a return address of *Something About Mary,* on the Fox Lot. No note or letter, just the cassette. I made repeated efforts to contact them without success. It was very unfulfilling to be left without a firm resolution.

I called the film critic of the Providence Journal to ask him how I should read this. He opined that the filmmaking industry is one of few winners and a lot of losers. The Farrellys had finally reached the winner's circle after putting in their time. There is nothing that would indicate that they would want to share a lifeboat without a benefit to themselves. This reality totally made sense and allowed me to let go of my altruistic idealism. I was now adapting to the new reality of me against the machine.

My new strategy was to make a list of all the mini-major and major studios. It is almost impossible to get through the gatekeepers at any of these organizations without a finished product. Scripts don't count. I happened to be bona fide, one step up the food-chain, because I possessed a finished film. They took my calls and asked for a copy. I was, once again, feeling like I was in the industry. I was talking to acquisition people, who expressed interest and made me feel like I might have a chance. Over the next year, I had made connections with every single studio acquisition department except DreamWorks.

DreamWorks happens to have the toughest gatekeeper. No one gets through without a connection. You pretty much have to have Spielberg's imprimatur. That's okay, I had a good number of real contacts everywhere else. The only problem was that, over time, they collectively rejected my film in similar wording, "It's not for us." This on the face means that they either don't know how to market it or they just didn't like it. I spoke to the film critic of the Providence Journal and asked for a read on this general style blow off. He said that even if a studio dislikes your work, they won't level with you and flat out reject it because they recognize that your next project may be a blockbuster, and you may not give them a look because they alienated you. It's just safest to tell you it isn't for them. In every case, I would query further to see if I could get an honest assessment. Some of the V.P.s would elaborate. Several said they liked my movie but asked why I didn't go with known actors. I jokingly would respond that I didn't think Tom Cruise would return my call. Sony pictures told me that they could spend a half million dollars promoting my film, but they doubted they would ever see their money back. Another V.P. said this was an urban tale with limited appeal. He didn't think mid-country farmers would get cleaned up and go to town to see my movie. My favorite comment of all was from a high-level V.P. at Paramount Pictures, whose name I recognized. His remark was, "Your movie is just like *Dumb and Dumber*." I was extremely flattered with that comment until he finished with, "I hated *Dumb and Dumber*." I challenged his view by citing that *Dumb and Dumber* was a box office hit. He said he was aware, but he still didn't like it and he was, after all, the decider on what got acquired.

My option list was shrinking, and my resolve was taking a hit. During this time of studio submissions, and my continuation of sending out benevolent checks to film festivals that wouldn't accept my film, the Farrellys were preparing to shoot their next film, *Me, Myself, and Irene,* near where I live. The newspaper told of their shooting schedule. They would be filming in downtown Jamestown, R.I.

I figured I would go and attempt to see Bobby

Farrelly and hopefully learn why he was incommunicado. I arrived at the shooting location and saw Bobby up ahead. I approached him, said hi, and waited to see if he remembered me. He did, and he asked how everything was going with my film. I responded that I had it out to all the studios and was awaiting responses. Then the strangest thing happened. I mentioned that I had my movie out to Fox, which was the studio they worked with. Well, the reflex reaction I saw on his face was of someone getting a root canal. His reaction was totally involuntary, and definitely total surprise. After a moment of absorption, Bobby then resumed with good luck wishes. In spite of the awkward moment, I asked if I could observe some of the shooting. He told me he would send someone out for me as he walked away toward the set. I waited a long time, but none ever came. That was the last time I would see or speak to Bobby Farrelly. I left the perimeter of the movie set dejected and fighting the emotion I felt.

There would be four other close encounters with Bobby Farrelly that would push the boundaries of mathematical probability. It was clear I wasn't going to get any assistance there, but to experience these close brushes was just a cruel reminder or wound opener. The first was during the shooting of *Irene*. I had become friends with a lady who, weeks later, told me that her daughter had recently met and was dating the Farrelly brothers' *Irene* producer, and that they were seeing each other regularly. Wonderful.

The second close encounter was during the Rhode Island Giant Slalom ski race that winter held at Wachusett Mountain. I had entered, skied my two runs, and had returned to the lodge rather late to check the results. On the results board, Bobby Farrelly's name was listed. I'd be damned. I searched through the lodge and couldn't find him. He must have left after the awards ceremony that I was late for.

The third came by way of one of my business customers who told me he still lived diagonally across from the home the Farrellys grew up in in Cumberland, RI. He related anecdotal stories of how the mischievous brothers would pull pranks on him, like releasing his caged pet chickens, or putting razor cut slits in his garden hose which would squirt all over the place when he needed hosed water. He couldn't hide his amusement or laughter when relating these funny memories.

The last encounter came when my personal care doctor gave me a referral to see a dermatologist in Fall River, MA. I arrived on the third floor of the medical building and discovered that my new dermatologist's office is next door to the Farrellys' mother's office. She had a nursing practice but was never in when I had my appointments.

Crossed paths but no resulting connection. I accepted the fate that my run of luck and fortune had run its course.

A few other near misses resulted during my push to find a distributor. My cousin, who travels extensively, informed me that he'd been dating a new girl. She was the executive secretary to the president of Showtime in New York City. What luck, a cable movie channel opportunity popped into my lap. My cousin introduced me to her, and she offered to give a copy of my movie to the president, which she did. Unfortunately, he passed. Near misses were becoming so routinely common in my world that I'd grown numb.

By that time, I was feeling very ground down in my quest for distribution. The film festival rejection letters were adding to my dismay. I seemed to be in a stalled position of arrested progress.

Up until then, all was moving ahead with a serendipitous charm. Then a wall. This couldn't be happening, could it?

Coinciding with my multi-pronged attempts to find a home for my baby, two filmmakers with a film budget close to mine were getting national buzz. Their film was going viral, before the term actually existed. *The Blair Witch Project* is a fictional tale that is presented as a possible non-fiction documentary. The story was about three filmmakers pursuing a legend of a witch in the woods of Maryland. They filmed part of their story until they went missing, with only their equipment and film discovered. Fake police reports were filed. Missing persons' posters were printed up and posted on college campuses that the film was to be shown at. The marketing was brilliant to say the least. The campaign was launched while the film was still in production. They used online media, which was a fairly new medium.

Film marketing had now entered a new era. Not being a tech guy, I was totally unaware of the paradigm shift that was taking place.

My focus was all about making my film. Marketing would be addressed somewhere after I was done. *Blair Witch* showed me that the making and marketing now ran in parallel, building demand and interest.

Blair Witch was made for $60,000 and premiered at the Sundance Film Festival on January 25, 1999.

It was to become the first widely released film marketed through the internet.

The fact that it went on to gross $250,000,000 worldwide made this an even more incredible story.

This news caused me to rethink what I had been doing to market my film. It was too late for the promotion prior to launch. That ship had sailed. How could I market my film after over a year of conventional approaches? This was new territory that wasn't researchable, so I felt as lost in the woods as the cast of *Blair Witch*.

Remarkable as many of these events were, not one could equal the biggest occurrence that totally derailed my efforts. My good friend and lawyer Jim Reilly had told me of his close relationship with David Angell, a classmate from his Providence College days. David Angell went on to become a successful Emmy Award winning television producer for the shows *Cheers, Frasier,* and *Wings*. Jim had told me that David's success allowed David and his wife Lynn to go on vacations around the world and bring along their friends to share the fun. Jim was telling me what a truly special individual David was. Several months after hearing this story, I had a dream that Jim had sent David a copy of my movie and David took a liking to it. When I awoke, the dream was on my mind. I told myself I would call Jim that night and ask if he could forward a copy of my movie to David. That day was September 11, 2001. Our world had changed that morning and my dream about my movie was the furthest thing from my mind.

Like most people in this country—throughout the world—I was glued to my television that night to learn what was happening. As the evening went on, there were more and more facts being put out as they became known. All the information that was released resulted in an amalgam of shocked, incomprehensible, heartbreaking, and depressing emotions. Just when you can't imagine anything eclipsing this combination of feelings, the local television affiliate lists the passenger list from the two American Airlines jetliners that left Logan Airport in Boston that morning that were flown into the World Trade Center Towers. On board the first plane to hit, American Airlines flight 11, was Lynn and David Angell.

I was seated when this came on the screen which is the only reason I didn't lose my legs and fall over. I cannot put into words what I felt at that moment. A thesaurus of adjectives couldn't capture it. After the initial shock wore down, questions swirled in my mind. What was the significance of this dream and why on this very day? What was this all about? The answer will never come, so it will remain one of the greatest mysteries that will ever touch my life.

This event was just one more incident that made this project appear to have some odd Karma surrounding it. Again, I'm not a superstitious guy, but you've got to wonder?

After a few years of writing countless checks for thousands of dollars for entry fees to film festivals that ultimately wouldn't accept my film, I threw my hands up. Financing film festivals worldwide wasn't my intended objective. (I do have rejection letters from Sundance, and the Cannes film festival. How many people can make that claim?)

Maybe a stronger man than I could have kept on going, but I had to take a break from the totally impassable wall that I was trying to scale.

I decided my break in the action would be in the form of my next screenplay. Screw Hollywood and the film festivals, I would work on another project to achieve my Hollywood dream. There were a few acquisition execs that declined my film but invited me to submit future projects. Wow, an open door for another shot! A consolation prize for *BOXedMAN*.

It was a nice thought but another mountain to climb. The first script was a romantic comedy or Rom-Com in film land speak. I worked on that for a better part of a year, until I grew unhappy with what I had, put it on a shelf, and started another.

My second script was a Farrelly Brothers' style comedy about two orphaned brothers. I completed this one and was satisfied with what I had.

This script would find its way to the people who invited me to do so.

There was only one problem, the job security of people in acquisitions is very tenuous at best. My guess is, if you buy too many duds, you don't stick around for long. Considering the fact that most films don't make their money back, you can draw your own conclusion. So, there I was, several years away from my conversations with people who were no longer there. My open-door invites were no longer pertinent. Some of their successors were open to reading my script, some were not.

The end result…there were no takers on my script. This is the expected result that most writers experience, so no, I was not crushed. Bummed, but not crushed.

24

Close But No Cigar

It was announced in the local papers that on Monday, January 27, 2003, the Brown University Creative Arts Council was to honor Martin Scorsese as "America's foremost living director." Which, to my way of thinking was a hell of a lot better than "foremost dead director." If you're going to be one, I'd go with living.

Pardon my digression.

The program had limited seating on a first-come first-served basis. Scorsese was to show a 20-minute film clip, speak about his work, then take questions from the audience. The program was to be moderated by powerhouse talent agent and past Disney President Michael Ovitz. This announcement got my wheels spinning once again.

I would have been first in line to experience

this presentation except for my higher priority. I would do anything to get a copy of my movie to Scorsese. I would not be able to pull this off from a seat in the auditorium. I needed to have a face-to-face hand-off. My La La Land dream plan was that he may like my movie and be helpful in marketing. Perhaps he might be flattered that I referenced him by name in the scene when Rick and Rod are talking in the bar.

This was perfect! It couldn't fail, I thought.

I plotted my strategy. I went to the Brown campus around the start time of the program.

I went around the back of the auditorium to an alleyway where a black limo with New York plates was parked.

I knew this was where Scorsese would exit the building and depart. I drove away and parked my car down the street from there. I then needed to position myself out of the sight of the limo driver to avoid unwanted suspicion but within monitoring view of the auditorium doors. I would be a liar if I didn't think STALKER and had thoughts of Mark David Chapman walking up to John Lennon. Creepy, but I'm not an assassin, just a desperate filmmaker trying to market his film. So, I laid in waiting for what seemed an eternity till the back doors swung open and Scorsese emerged. He walked toward the limo as I simultaneously walked toward him with a measured pace to intercept him before he reached the limo's open door. My pulse quickened as I drew closer and closer to this familiar famous director. I was sweating bullets that someone would grab me and wrestle me to the ground. I don't recall how I addressed him, Martin, Marty, Mr. Scorsese. I rambled how I was a huge fan, and that I made a film that I thought he may like to see. He took my videocassette and entered the limo.

I left the alleyway with an incredible sense of accomplishment and relief that I wasn't wrestled to the ground by any security people. That was a very gutsy and potentially fatal strategy, but I was desperate. My La La Land fantasy was that he would, at the very least, send me a note saying good job and good luck.

I never did hear back from Scorsese, so for all I know, my video cassette ended up in a rest stop trash barrel on the way back to New York City. So much for that one person that believes in my project. I felt destined to be an industry outsider.

Okay, I rationalized, time for plan C (I truly never anticipated even a plan B).

I would write a memoir (which you are presently holding) about the making of the film.

An all-in-one tutorial on independent, guerrilla-style filmmaking, and an inspirational tale of taking a leap outside your comfort zone to pursue a dream.

This now seems like the most satisfying and obtainable goal that I will realistically attain.

Writing this book was satisfying, and a wonderful nostalgic trip down memory lane.

Pouring over the production records brought back all the incredible memories of a collaborative experience that was just the greatest experience of my life.

I wrote the majority of this book, up until I ran out of gas. I got to the point that I wasn't sure what I wanted to say, so I put this on the shelf.

Wow, these creative endeavors have a way of wearing you down, or at least me.

Not long after the shelving of this book, my Army Reserve unit was mobilized to train mobilized National Guard units for the wars in Iraq and Afghanistan. I was in a unit that was a Battle Command Training Group. Our assignment was to train units for security force missions in both war zones. My unit was sent to Ft. Dix in New Jersey for an 18-month assignment.

As I drove over the George Washington bridge to my new home for the next 18 months, I would look south across the Hudson River to lower Manhattan. I would see the empty skyline where the World Trade Center Twin Towers once stood, and I understood why I was making the trip. Politics aside as to the why and how we were involved in these conflicts, the bottom line was we were committed, and the support and training of our soldiers was paramount.

Anything you do in life, you seed it compared to prior life experiences. In that metric, I would have to put my trainer, mentor experience at the very top of the list.

Training soldiers for life or death situations is about as serious as you can get, and I took my mission seriously. My assignment was to be an imbedded trainer with a newly activated company (150-200 soldiers) for their two months train up before they deployed to the war zones.

This operation was so involving and intense that working on this book was not even a thought.

Every two months, I received a new unit and ran the same program, but with required adjustments that were fed back from the prior trained units in the war zones.

The two-month rotation allowed for enough of a together period to create a familial relationship. It was very natural to develop a kinship with the group of soldiers that would eventually part with me and advance to their one-year tour of duty in Iraq or Afghanistan. The reports from Iraq were not good, with suicide bombers and roadside bombs killing our soldiers daily. The troops we were training were heading into that chaotic mess with the goal of stemming the violence. My deepest wish was that they would all return safely to their family and friends unharmed. This was always on my mind, as the reports from Iraq continued to be dour.

Another new life perspective to experience and process. Making my film was a seven-month-long, totally focused experience, which I thought at the time was monumental. Now I was involved and committed to an eighteen-month-long, totally focused experience. This one though had a life and death component to it. Perspective indeed.

At the tail end of my mentor, trainer duty at Fort Dix, someone left a review of *BOXedMAN* on the IMDb website. (IMDb is the Internet Movie Data base website, where all movies made are listed.)

The quote read, "Local comedian, Ace Aceto, in the lead role, had a big following in the RI area. The producers picked him up when he was hot and recognizable. We were hoping his career would take off after this film."

Ace called me to make me aware of his newly discovered impertinence. I could tell he was stung by the comment. I remind him of Mark Twain's quote, "The reports of my death are greatly exaggerated." We were both re-feeling the lack of love.

By the time I finished my 18 months, I had all I could do to get my former life back in order.

I am a sales rep for a corrugated box company, and the market condition I returned to was not a good one. The company I worked for, which was a Fortune 500 company, was going through major changes. My accounts were in disarray due to corporate plant consolidations. I was losing accounts due to poor service and other complications. Then the business meltdown of 2008 added to the misery.

Murphy's law says this isn't challenging enough, so let's have the company file for Chapter 11 a year later to make this situation ever more dire. Finishing my book was the furthest thing from my mind. My livelihood was in the balance. I did all I could do to keep my head above water in the subsequent years.

In 2013, a layoff opened a new door. This led to my present position with the company whose box shop I used in the movie. They were named Action Container at that time but are presently Abbott-Action (changes are part of life). It's a breath of fresh air when you go from the pressure cooker of the corporate world to a privately-owned company without all the negative stuff.

My new position at Abbott-Action Inc. has allowed me to work without all the pressures and problems I had been under. I now work for an amazing company that can run circles around my former mega corporation. I was now in a position to have a clear mind in my spare time to complete my book.

There's lot to be said for mental health. Not to pontificate, but, if you are in an unhealthy situation, make it your mission to get out...ASAP. We all deserve to not be mistreated or abused.

Completing this book has put the closing punctuation mark on this totally incredible experience. *BOXedMAN* is far from a perfect film, but it is relatable to anyone who has worked in sales or had a jerk for a boss. I can imagine the number of hands going up.

I hope I have also inspired some to take that step off the ledge to chase that yearning desire. Although I didn't make it to Hollywood, the memories and existence of my film marks an accomplishment that I will be forever proud of.

I hope you enjoyed it and had some laughs.

Nick Pasyanos

P.S. The following screenplay is what was used to film from.

Any changes in wording in the film was done on location as the actors saw fit.

Improvised dialog was encouraged from the cast.

I had used my name as the protagonist's when writing but revised to Rick for filming.

25

The Screenplay

EXT. COLLEGE CAMPUS PLAYING FIELD - DAY

The playing field is filled with students and parents seated in chairs, listening to the commencement speaker's speech.

NICK (V. O.)

Someone recently asked me about my apparent good fortune in life. I asked him what he meant. He replied, "You're successful in your work and you have such a positive outlook on life. Happy and successful, what else is there? Most of us would be lucky to get one of them right." I answered, "My life didn't start out that way. Happiness and success are destinations that you're aware of only after you've arrived." His next question was: "How did you get there?" I reflected back in time to determine where to start my story. I think this is probably as good a place as any.

EXT. PLAYING FIELD PODIUM - DAY

Graduating students walk up to the podium in a steady flow, receiving their diplomas as their names are announced.

EXT. GARDEN COCKTAIL RECEPTION - DAY

Parents and students in caps and gowns converse in groups throughout the garden. A grandmother works her way through the crowd apparently searching for someone. Her gaze seems fixed. She then smiles and raises her hand.

GRANDMOTHER

Nicky! Nicky! Over here!

Several yards away, a young man in cap and gown turns in the direction of his grandmother's voice and raises his hand in acknowledgment.

NICK

Grandma!

Nick makes his way through the crowd to where his grandmother stands. Nick throws his arms around her and kisses her cheek.

NICK

Gram, you made it. I'm so glad. You really worried me when you told me you weren't well. You look great! Is everything OK?

Nick's grandmother looks away so her reaction doesn't betray her.

GRANDMOTHER
(halfheartedly)

I feel fine. Everything is fine.

Nick's grandmother turns her face toward him again and with a renewed composure.

GRANDMOTHER

Nicky, did you really think I would miss your graduation? I may not be feeling well, but the Lord would have to claim me before I'd miss this day.

Nick's grandmother holds his face between her hands. Her face beams with pride.

GRANDMOTHER

You're the first person from our family to attend and graduate from college. This is the proudest moment of my life.

NICK

Please, Grandma, don't pile it on. Let's not forget that I am also the oldest graduating person in my class. In fact, I may be the oldest person to graduate from this school.

GRANDMOTHER

Nicky, it isn't your fault that you needed a little more time to decide what you wanted to do.

NICK

A little more time? Ten years is hardly a little more time. Besides, I still don't know what I want to do.

GRANDMOTHER

The tough times are behind you now. You got your head together, you went to school and now you've graduated. I'm so happy! The Lord can take me now, I'm ready. I don't need to live another moment or experience another event. My life's fulfilled.

NICK

Grandma, stop that talk. You'll live a lot longer than you think. Stop talking like that.

GRANDMOTHER

All right, I'm sorry. I'm just so happy.

She reflects for a moment and then continues.

GRANDMOTHER

I only wish your parents could be here also.

Nick stares at her with a look of mixed emotions.

NICK

But they're not, and you are, so let's enjoy this day. We've got some celebrating to do.

Nick puts his arm around his grandmother as they walk toward one of the punchbowls. He pours two glasses of punch and hands his grandmother one. Nick and his grandmother touch their glasses together, toasting one another.

GRANDMOTHER

Where's this wonderful girl you've been seeing? Kathleen, isn't it?

NICK

Uh, yeah, Kathy. (pause) Well, we sort of had a fight, er, disagreement last night, so she decided not to come today.

Nick's grandmother looks quizzically at him, as if in search of a more credible explanation for Kathy's absence.

NICK

She was really mad. She has an uncontrollable temper. You don't know.

GRANDMOTHER

What did you do to anger her so?

NICK

Actually, I'm not sure. It was an escalation of another meaningless fight three days ago.

Nick's grandmother looks sympathetically at him.

NICK

It's okay. I've gotten used to it. I really haven't had much luck with women. Believe it or not, Kathy is a big improvement from my last girlfriend. So in that respect, I'm making progress.

Nick's grandmother looks at him and touches his cheek affectionately.

INT. APARTMENT LIVING ROOM NIGHT

A party is in full swing. Young men and women are celebrating their graduation. A keg of beer in a barrel of ice is at the front door. Nick and his friend, Rod, are speaking to each other in a corner of the room. (Opposite from the side of the room where the stereo speakers are blaring)

ROD

Well, my man, we made it.
(Raising his hand to high five)

NICK

Yeah, pinch me.
(Making palm to palm high five contact)

ROD

I won't need a pinch. My wake up call will be tomorrow. That's when my old man will start building the pressure. What are you going to do? Are you sending out resumes? How are you going to pay your school loans? Do you have any idea of what field you'll enter? Aw shit, I can hear it now. You don't know how lucky you are not to have to listen to all that crap.

• • •

Nick looks at Rod with surprise at his comment.

ROD

I'm sorry. That was pretty insensitive of me. But you know what I mean.

NICK

Yeah, forget about it.

ROD

What the hell was I talking about before I stepped on my dick?

NICK

Your concern over your old man chewing your ass about your future job.

ROD

Yeah, right. Truth is, I don't know what I'm going to do.

Nick chuckles at Rod's honesty.

ROD

Very funny. And I suppose you know what you're going to do?

NICK

No, I don't, but you can bet your ass it'll be something that pays a lot. My first priority is to get my grandmother out of that retirement home, before she dies of depression.

ROD

Why is she there again?

NICK

She lost her house after my grandfather died. A long illness without health and life insurance will do it every time. She misses her own place so much, she's miserable. She doesn't say so, but I know so.

(CONTINUED)

(MORE)

NICK (CONT'D)

First and foremost, I've got to get my grandmother's life back. You know, her independence and dignity. That's the very least I owe her. I need a job that pays big and fast.

ROD

Oh, sure. What are you going in to, investment banking? This isn't the eighties you know.

(chuckling)

NICK

Actually, I've been giving serious consideration to some sort of sales.

Rod looks amazed.

ROD

Sales? You want to be a piece of shit used car salesman? Say it ain't so.

NICK

It ain't so! I'm talking about selling serious shit, industrial, technical, investment. Something noble. Not fucking used cars. Give me some credit. (pauses) Used car salesman? (Shaking his head)

Nick shakes his head in disbelief at the thought of Rod misjudging him.

NICK

Actually, I might be closer to a job than you think. I've got an appointment downtown with a head-hunter Tuesday. We're going to go over all my options.

ROD
(Shaking his head)

Salesman?

NICK

Hey, some salesmen earn a pretty good living.

Nick speaks the words in a manner that sounds like he's trying to convince himself.

ROD

I'm gonna be downtown Tuesday night. Let's meet at Griswolds at 6:00. I can't wait to see what you're going to come up with.

EXT. GRISWOLDS RESTAURANT - DAY

. . .

Heavy traffic flows in front of the restaurant.

INT. GRISWOLDS RESTAURANT - DAY

Nick and Rod are seated at the bar, talking.

ROD

Three interviews.

NICK
(Confirming nod)

Three interviews.

ROD

Give me that guy's card. Maybe I can land a job before my old man starts ragging on me. What kind of companies are they?

NICK

Two are industrial suppliers, and one is a corrugated box company.

ROD

Corrugated box company?

(Quizzically)

NICK

You know, cardboard boxes.

ROD

Cardboard boxes? You'd consider selling something that grocery stores give away?

NICK

Sure, every manufacturer that makes anything has to put the product in a box. Everybody needs them. How hard can it be?

• • •

EXT. OFFICE OF ROCK BOX - DAY

Nick is walking up the walkway to the office.

INT. RECEPTION AREA OF ROCK BOX - DAY

Nick walks up to the reception desk.

NICK

I'm here to see Mr. Edward Moss.

RECEPTIONIST

And your name?

NICK

Nick Williams. He's expecting me.

• • •

The operator calls Mr. Moss's line.

OPERATOR

Mr. Moss, Mr. Williams is here to see you.

INT. EDWARD MOSS'S OFFICE - DAY

EDWARD

So Nick, that's what I have to offer. I feel it's a very competitive compensation and benefit plan.

There's something in Edward's voice that comes across as insincere. There's also a quirkiness in his subtle mannerisms that tells Nick that maybe Mr. Moss may not be totally comfortable with the claims he's just made.

EDWARD

And remember, the harder you work, the more you can make. There's no limit to the income you can earn.

. . .

The strangeness of his delivery comes through again. With the visit apparently at an end, Nick rises and shakes Edward's hand.

NICK

Well, thank you very much for the offer, Mr. Moss. Could I have a day or two to think it over?

EDWARD

Of course, of course. This is a big step for you, but I know you'll work out fine. I can tell a go getter when I see one.

EXTERIOR. PHONE BOOTH ON STREET - DAY

NICK

Kathy.. Hi. It's me. You won't believe. I got the job... Well, I didn't accept yet, but they want me. (Pause) Yeah, it was the box company. I didn't go to the other two. Industrial supplies just doesn't sound glamorous enough.

KATHY (V.O)

Oh, and cardboard boxes are glamorous? Are you whacked out or something? I thought you were going to get a real job.

NICK

This is a real job. The income potential is great. Hey, everybody uses them.

KATHY (V.O.)
(Sarcastically)

Well, I'm very happy for you.

NICK

Listen, I'm meeting Rod at Griswolds at six. Why don't you meet me there and we'll have dinner and celebrate?

KATHY (V.O.)

I'll pass. You know I don't like Rod.

NICK

I know, but for that matter, you don't like any of my friends.

KATHY (V.O.)

Says a lot about your taste in people.

NICK

Okay, okay, I've had enough. You know where I'll be if you change your mind... See you tomorrow. Bye.

Nick hangs-up the phone, shakes his head and walks away.

EXT. GRISWOLDS RESTAURANT - DAY

• • •

Rod is waiting outside. Nick arrives and the two go in together.

INT. GRISWOLDS RESTAURANT - DAY

ROD

So, how'd it go today?

NICK

Well, I got a job.

ROD

You got a job? I thought it was an interview?

NICK

It was, but the general manager at the box company must have liked me because he talked to me for almost three hours, and then he made me an offer. He must have seen something in me.

ROD

Yeah, the fact that he can get you cheap.

NICK

Nah. I think he recognized something in me. I certainly don't know what it is because I'm not really sure I can sell. I'm actually pretty scared right now. I've never really had much self confidence, and this job requires it in spades. I haven't accepted the job yet... the manager has given me a day to decide, so I can still back out.

ROD

Is it a good job?

NICK

Yeah, it's a really good job, company car, expense account, and unlimited income potential.

ROD

I'll kick your ass if you don't accept this job. Are you fucking nuts? I'm surprised that you didn't blow the boss.

NICK

He wasn't my type. All kidding aside, I'm really afraid. I'm not good in pressure situations, where I'm expected to come through.

ROD

You'll do fine. You just have to have a serious talk with your negative inner self. Speaking of negative, have you told Kathy?

NICK

Yeah. And you called it. Negative. Shit, every time I need emotional support or just a little encouragement, she bails out on me.

ROD

Well, why don't you bail on her? Who needs that aggravation? What do you get out of your relationship, other than occasional sex?

NICK

I guess that might be it. And it's getting less occasional.

ROD

Why not meet someone else?

NICK

You talk like this is an everyday occurrence. Meet someone else. Thanks for the tip. You've obviously forgotten our past talks about how difficult it is meeting women, and how much I hate the whole process. I'd rather stay right where I am, thanks.

ROD

Suit yourself.

NICK

Say, I've been wanting to see the new Scorcese picture for the past three weeks, and Kathy doesn't want to go. Do you want to go?

ROD

I'm really tired and I don't think I can stay awake.

NICK

Come on, you know once you get into it, you won't fall asleep. It's Scorcese!

ROD

OK, but only because I feel sorry for you. I still say ditch the bitch.

INT. MOVIE THEATER - NIGHT

• • •

Nick and Rod are seated together approximately mid- theater. Every seat is filled. The movie is in progress. Nick and Rod are sharing the popcorn and candy that they collectively bought. A girl with a date is seated next to Rod. She keeps looking over at Rod & Nick with a curious stare. Nick picks up on her glances and starts to fidget in response to the girl's stare.

INT. MOVIE THEATER - NIGHT

Rod is now falling asleep during the movie. His head falls over onto Nick's shoulder. This doesn't go unnoticed by the girl next to Rod, who seems very amused by this apparent act of affection between Rod and Nick. Meanwhile, Nick is getting very agitated as he repeatedly elbows Rod in the ribs to get him off his shoulder. After repeated tries, Rod's head continues to fall on Nick's shoulder. The girl seated next to Rod now has clued her date in on the two sweethearts next to her.

The girl and her date are both now so amused by Rod and Nick that they aren't paying attention to the movie. A frustrated Nick now gives Rod one more elbow to the ribs.

NICK
(Whispering)

ROD!

The girl and her date turn to each other with eyebrows raised, grinning wildly at what they just heard.

GIRL

It must be loverboy's nickname.

EXT. CITY STREET - NIGHT

Rod and Nick are walking together.

NICK

I'll never forgive your ass for that display in the theater. Did you see that couple looking at us? They thought we were a couple of homos. Like I don't have enough problems without going through something like that.

ROD

Well, I won't forgive you either if you don't accept that job tomorrow. You have to take it.

NICK

You know I'm going to take it. I don't think I can do it, but I can't let the chance pass me by, I've gotta help my grandmother.

ROD

That's the spirit.

NICK

I'm still not forgiving your ass for tonight. What if they ever see us again?

ROD

You're too damn sensitive, lighten up.

INT. OFFICE - DAY

Edward Moss is walking down a corridor with Nick. Edward opens a door marked Sample Room. They enter a large room with sample boxes on display. Edward leads Nick to the desk of the designer.

EDWARD

Steve, this is Nick Williams. Nick is joining us as a sales rep. I'd like him to spend a week with you to learn the ropes.

Then he'll spend two weeks with a few of our salesmen to see how they work. And after that, we unleash him on the world.

STEVE

Great.

Steve extends his hand to welcome Nick.

NICK

Pleased to meet you.

EDWARD starts to walk away, then stops and turns around.

EDWARD

Oh Steve, could you please take Nick out to the plant and give him a tour. I'm short on time today.

STEVE

Sure, Edward. No problem.

Edward waves a thanks and continues walking to the door out of the sample room. Edward exits the room.

NICK

Does he only go by Edward?

STEVE

Only by Edward. Not Ed. Only Edward. He's very anal about that.

NICK

Thanks for clueing me in.

STEVE

That's okay. Actually, there's a lot of things that you need some forewarning on.

Nick looks at Steve with a look of surprise.

NICK

For instance?

STEVE

Are you related to Edward?

NICK
(Looking puzzled)

No.

STEVE

Did you know him prior to being hired?

NICK
(Still puzzled)

No. I just met him at the interview.

STEVE

Good, then I can tell you candidly that Edward is dumb like a stick.

NICK

He is?

STEVE

He came to us from General Motors. He was a crash test dummy there.

Nick breaks up laughing.

STEVE

That was an excuse he just made about not having time to show you around. Truth is, he doesn't know anything about what goes on behind that wall.

Steve points at the wall that separates the sample room from the factory.

NICK

How did he ever get the job he has?

STEVE

Easy. Lucky sperm club. His old man was a wheel with the company years ago. But it's interesting, Edward doesn't acknowledge any of those facts. Basically, he was born on third base and he thinks he hit a triple.

NICK
(Sarcastically)

This is great. Any other juicy info I should know?

STEVE

Frankly, I don't know where to start. Everybody here hates him. He manages through intimidation. He's either threatening you, or screwing you. Last year, a few of us got together and had these made up.

Steve reaches into the bottom drawer of his desk and pulls out a T-shirt that he proceeds to unfold and hold up for Nick to read. The inscription in bold type: YOU CAN'T SCARE ME, I WORK FOR EDWARD MOSS. Nick's expression goes from amusement to concern as he absorbs the words.

NICK (V.O.)

So this was my introduction to the business world. Here I am fresh out of school, insecure as hell, and I find myself working for an airhead with a mean streak. I think this is a dangerous combination. Maybe this box selling idea wasn't so great after all.

STEVE

Have you met the other salesmen yet?

NICK

No. But I will tomorrow. Moss is sending me out with each to see how they work.

Steve rolls his eyes, looks at the floor and lets out a chuckle.

STEVE

That's what I'd like to know.

NICK

Huh?

STEVE

I'd like to know what makes them work.

Nick looks at Steve with an expression of non comprehension.

INT. ENTRY DOOR TO EDWARD'S OFFICE - DAY

Nick reaches in and knocks on the open door. Edward Moss is sitting at his desk with an elderly man sitting across from him. Edward rises and walks over to greet Nick at the door.

EDWARD

Nick. Please come in. I'd like you to meet Ed Walsh.

Nick walks over to Ed and shakes his hand.

EDWARD

Ed is our most senior sales rep. A real pro. You won't find a harder worker or more successful salesman. He'll show you the road to success.

NICK

I'm looking forward to working with you.

Nick is demonstrably enthused at meeting this successful veteran.

NICK (V.O.)

This was a pretty exciting moment for me. Ed's build- up was so inspirational. Inspirational until I'd spent two days with him.

INT. ED WALSH'S CAR - DAY

• • •

Nick is riding in the passenger side as Ed Walsh is driving and talking non stop about nothing. Nick is noticeably bored.

ED

Amazing, isn't it?

NICK

Yeah, it sure is.

It's apparent that Nick doesn't know what Ed's talking about. Ed looks down at his wristwatch.

ED

How about a coffee? It's ten o'clock already.

NICK

Sure.

. . .

Ed pulls off the road to a roadside diner.

INT. DINER - DAY

Nick and Ed enter the diner. A waitress behind the counter greets Ed and Nick as the two take adjoining stools.

WAITRESS

Good morning, Ed. You have a sidekick today?

ED

Yes. He's my new protégé. I'm breaking him in. You know, showing him the ropes.

The waitress turns to Nick.

WAITRESS

Well, good luck to you. You've got a great guy to work with.

• • •

The waitress turns her attention to Ed.

WAITRESS

What'll it be, Ed? The regular?

ED

Of course, and a duplicate for my friend here.

INT. ED'S CAR - DAY

Ed and Nick are riding together with Ed talking non-stop again. Ed looks at his watch.

ED

It's twenty to twelve, too late to visit anyone now. Let's go to lunch. I hope you don’t mind if I pick the restaurant?

• • •

Nick nods his head in agreement.

ED

I only eat at restaurants that serve health foods. People don't realize the importance of eating wholesome and healthy foods. Good foods are good for the bowels, and you can't neglect your bowels. I have warmed prunes every morning to purge my digestive system and hot coffee a couple of times a day to finish the job. With a cleaned out system like that, It'd be a sin to eat anything but natural wholesome foods. Good foods going through a clean system is what I always say.

NICK (V.O.)

In all honesty, my two days with Ed were not what I would describe as inspirational. Between telling me about his health concerns and stopping for his mandatory health food lunches and mid morning and afternoon coffee breaks, I honestly don't know how he gets anything done.

INT. ED'S CAR - DAY

. . .

Ed and Nick are riding together with Ed still talking about health matters.

ED

So, I told him, hey, it's my health, you know!

Ed looks down at his watch.

ED

Wow! It's two thirty already. I could really go for a coffee.

INT. EDWARD MOSS'S OFFICE - DAY

Edward is introducing Nick to a middle-aged man who is impeccably dressed, as though he just came off a page of G.Q. Nick's eyes scan him quickly, noticing details, such as the monogrammed cuff links and the silk handkerchief in the chest pocket.

EDWARD

Nick, I'd like you to met Frank Casters. Frank has been with us for years. A real professional! A few days with Frank will help you immeasurably. He has connections like no other.

INT. FRANK'S CAR - DAY

Frank is driving, postured as though he were modeling for an automobile advertisement. His actions are very deliberate, almost robot like and he speaks in a monotonous tone of voice.

FRANK

The people we'll be visiting today are corporate buyers of some of the best known companies in America. I have very good relationships with the decision makers in these companies. In fact I know the Presidents and Vice Presidents in many of these companies.

• • •

INT. OFFICE LOBBY - DAY

Frank and Nick enter the lobby of an office which is very elegant. Glass and chrome are everywhere. Nick's eyes are moving left and right, trying to take it all in as they move toward the reception desk. Frank takes out a business card and introduces himself.

FRANK

Good morning, we're here to see Jeff Lerner.

RECEPTIONIST

Do you have an appointment?

FRANK

No, but he knows me.

RECEPTIONIST

He's on a call right now. If you'll have a seat, I'll contact him as soon as his line is clear.

FRANK

Thanks.

Nick and Frank walk over to the glass outer wall to wait for the receptionist. Frank immediately starts looking at his image in the glass. Frank fidgets with his tie, his shirt cuffs, and the tail of his impeccably tailored double breasted jacket.

INT. JEFF LERNER'S OFFICE - DAY

Frank and Nick are seated in front of Jeff Lerner's desk. Frank is talking and his voice is as monotonous as it was in the car earlier.

FRANK

I'm going to speak to our principals and see what kind of offer we can make. I can't see any reason why you can't do all your business with us. After all, we are the best.

Jeff and Nick are very apparently bored with Frank's monotonous sales pitch. Frank continues speaking with an air of superiority.

NICK (V.O.)

Frank was all you could loath in a salesman. He was pompous and arrogant. He spoke as though he was above you. How he became successful, I'll never know.

(CONTINUED)

(MORE)

NICK (CONT'D)

I don't think his customers even like him. I still can't make any sense of all this. So far, I haven't seen anything admirable about Rock Box's sales force, that is, until I met Bob Wish.

• • •

INT. EDWARD MOSS'S OFFICE - DAY

Edward Moss once again is introducing Nick to a middle aged salesman sitting in his office. The salesman seated is very average in appearance and dress.

EDWARD

Nick, this is Bob Wish.

Nick shakes Bob's hand.

NICK

Pleased to meet you.

EDWARD

Bob is second-most senior rep.

. . .

Edward pauses, as if he has nothing more to say about Bob. There's an uncomfortable silence before he continues.

EDWARD

Bob is someone you might learn something from.

It's apparent from the lack of accolades that Edward isn't as fond of Bob as he is his other salesmen.

EDWARD

You should have a good few days with Bob.

Edward's delivers the words without conviction or feelings.

INT. BOB WISH'S CAR - DAY

BOB

How the hell did you ever choose this business? You graduate from school, the world is your oyster, and you find yourself in the box business. Rock Box, no less.

NICK

The way I see it, everyone uses them, so I thought, how hard can it be? Selling boxes should be easy.

BOB

That's what you think. Did it occur to you to ask anyone how many competitors we have?

Nick displays a quizzical look and as he opens his mouth to speak.

BOB

I'll save you having to answer. Of course, you didn't.

Nick nods affirmatively.

BOB

Well, first of all, your observation about everyone using them is correct. That's as much as I'll give you credit for. You flunk the rest of the test. You see, there are more people selling boxes in this market than you want to know about. And coincidentally, the business base is shrinking, so you have too many companies trying to share a shrinking pie. You'll have your work cut out for you.

NICK

So how do Ed Morris and Frank Casters manage?

Bob laughs out loud at Nick's question.

BOB

Those two stiffs? Well, there's a story to both of them. Ed, as you know, is older than dirt. He's been doing this his whole life. Over the years he's built an account base that allows him to drink coffee and eat nuts, berries, and wheat germ all day. His only concerns are that he shits enough times each day. You've probably figured that out by now.

Nick nods affirmatively, with a smile.

BOB

And Frank, well, that's too weird for fiction. Before Frank started here, we had a super salesman who had all Frank's accounts. He retired, so Edward went out interviewing and of all the people he could have hired, he picks that hollow piece of shit.

NICK

What do you think he saw in him?

BOB

Easy answer. A facade. Edward is too stupid to see through Frank's facade. Edward is a sucker for that empty crap like silk hankies and monogrammed cufflinks.

Bob reaches down and grabs a piece of paper next to him and holds it up full face to Nick.

BOB

Frank and Edward are just like this piece of paper, looks substantial when you look at it. But...

Bob now rotates the piece of paper so its edge faces Nick.

BOB

This is what's really there under closer examination. Nothing. They're both losers. No substance.

NICK

So what's your story?

BOB

Me, no story really. I'm just a survivor. I know what I've got to do, and I do it. My best tip to you is to build good relationships with your contacts. Do favors for them any chance you get. That's what'll make you a survivor.

NICK

You do stuff like that?

BOB

You bet your ass. Why I've gone as far as hiring a limo and a hooker for a customer.

Nick looks incredulous.

NICK

You did?

BOB

It really wasn't a big deal. I have a customer who told me his wife won't screw him anymore, and he was considering a hooker. Well, I have a good friend with a limo service who knows people in (his eyebrows raise) escort services. So I set it up. He's been eternally grateful to me, even though the night didn't turn out quite right.

NICK

What happened?

BOB

Well, you see, Pete had a little too much to drink that night.

INT. BACK SEAT OF A LIMOUSINE - NIGHT

A heavy set man is sitting in the back seat in a drunken state. A blond haired woman's head is bobbing up and down in his lap. He suddenly lurches forward causing the blond to fall over onto the floor. The man starts knocking on the glass that separates the driver's compartment from the back.

MAN

Stop the car! Stop the car! I'm gonna get sick!

EXT. INTERSTATE 95 - NIGHT

The limousine suddenly pulls over into the break-down lane, the back door opens, and the heavy set man stumbles out of the car with his pants around his ankles. The man bends over and starts throwing up while the blond haired woman sits at the open door watching him. The headlights of passing cars illuminate the scene.

BOB (V.O.)

So, there's Pete, outside the limo, puking his guts out while the hooker watches.

NICK (V.O.)

Oh, man. Could there be anything more embarrassing? What about your friend the chauffeur? What did he think?

BOB (V.O.)

Think? He wasn't thinking anything. He was busy helping pull Pete's pants up.

EXT. HIGHWAY BREAKDOWN LANE - NIGHT

The chauffeur's hands are visible, pulling up Pete's pants and underwear. Pete can be heard, still retching. The headlights of the passing cars illuminate the scene.

INT. BOB WISH'S CAR - DAY

Nick is laughing so hard he's wiping tears from his eyes. Bob points his finger at a building up ahead.

BOB

This is Pete's company. You can meet the man right now.

INT. PETE'S OFFICE - DAY

Nick and Bob enter Pete's office. Pete very enthusiastically meets them, shaking Bob's hand.

PETE

Hey, how've you been?

BOB

Great, good to see you. I'd like you to meet Nick Williams.

Pete turns to Nick and shakes his hand.

PETE

Good to meet you. Are you replacing Bob?

BOB

Fuck you, wise ass. No, Nick just joined our company and he's spending a few days with me to see how I work.

PETE

Pay attention, Nick. Bob is the best and he won't steer you wrong. A real straight shooter. (beat). Kinda reminds me of myself. (beat). Straight as they come.

Nick and Bob look at each other with the telling smiles of people who share an inside joke. Pete picks up on the glances. After several looks at Nick and Bob,

Pete runs his hand down his face and looks at the floor as he shakes his head, smiling.

PETE

You just can't let me forget, can you?

Pete looks at Nick.

PETE

But it only happened once.

INT. BOB WISH'S CAR - DAY

BOB

So, you break your cherry tomorrow?

NICK

Yup.

BOB

Have you scoped out your territory?

NICK

I've been making a list of prospects from directories.

BOB

You've got just about virgin territory. Your territory has been too far for me to travel to, too unglamorous for Frank's elitist taste, and lacks the public toilet facilities that Ed requires.

Nick chuckles at Bob's observations.

BOB

Hey, with all this business talk, I never asked you if you're married.

NICK

No, thank God. With my shitty luck with women, I couldn't tolerate a steady diet of hell.

BOB

Been that lucky, huh?

NICK

Yeah. (unhappily)

BOB

Me too.

NICK

You married?

BOB

I was. (beat) Then she left me.

NICK

Sorry.

BOB

It's okay. It's been several years now and I've fully adjusted. It was tough though. I have to credit my customers for getting me through. They really were great. I've formed some great friendships during the lowest point of my life. My customers became my social circle, my confidants, Christ, they became my family. They're now my life. They're all I've got. Is it any wonder that I love my job so much?

NICK

I hope I meet with similar success.

BOB

You'll do just fine. Tomorrow the big day, huh?

NICK

Yea, I'm soloing. No parachute.

BOB

Best of luck, buddy.

INT. NICK'S CAR - DAY

• • •

Nick is driving while studying a map in his lap. He is lost and appears frazzled. He looks ahead and sees a gas station. He drives his car into the station.

EXT. GAS STATION - DAY

An Indian man walks up to Nick's car. Nick turns to the man.

NICK

Excuse me, but could you please tell me where Cooper Wire is?

INDIAN MAN

Oooh. I do not know this place.

NICK

It's in Montville.

INDIAN MAN

I do not know this place.

NICK

Cooper Wire or Montville?

INDIAN MAN

I am not familiar.

NICK

Never mind.

INDIAN MAN

Very good, yes?

Nick puts his car in drive and pulls out of the station frustrated.

• • •

INT. NICK'S CAR - DAY

Nick continues driving, simultaneously reading his map. He sees a variety store ahead. He pulls up and parks in front.

INT. VARIETY STORE - DAY

Nick walks up to the man behind the counter who is Indian.

NICK

Excuse me. Could you please tell me where Cooper Wire is?

INDIAN MAN

Ooohh, this I do not know.

NICK

Is this Montville?

INDIAN MAN

Montville?

He gestures with his hand in a waving action.

INDIAN MAN

Very, very far away.

NICK

How far?

INDIAN MAN

Too far.

EXT. VARIETY STORE - DAY

• • •

Nick exits the store, gets back into his car, and drives out of the parking lot. Less than a block away, he sees the signs for Cooper Wire. Nick shakes his head in disbelief.

INT. PROSPECT'S LOBBY - DAY

Nick walks up to the receptionist and hands his business card to her.

NICK

Would it be possible to see the person that buys boxes for your company?

INT. PROSPECT'S OFFICE - DAY

Nick walks in and shakes the hand of the man who greets him.

NICK

Nick Williams. Rock Box. Nice to meet you, Roger.

ROGER

Same here. Have a seat.

Roger motions to Nick to take a seat. Roger goes back to his seat behind his desk.

ROGER

Tell me about Rock Box.

Roger slinks down into his chair as if in preparation of a long, drawn out story.

NICK

Well, Rock Box is a company that's been in business for over 40 years..

NICK (V.O.)

I couldn't tell if Roger was paying attention to me or not. First, he looked dazed. Then his eyes were darting left and right as though he was trying to follow a fly. The worst was yet to come.

Roger is slumping even more now. his attention is apparently gone, and he's starting to pick his teeth with Nick's business card.

NICK (V.O)

I can't believe what I'm seeing. This asshole is picking his teeth with my card. He's desecrating my card!

INT. OFFICE LOBBY - DAY

Nick walks up to a receptionist, handing her his card.

NICK

Hi. My name is Nick Williams, from Rock Box. Would it be possible to see the person that buys boxes for your company?

RECEPTIONIST

Hold on please.

The receptionist keys in on her switchboard.

RECEPTIONIST

Ron, could you see Nick Williams from Rock Box?

The receptionist nods her head as she listens to Ron on the phone.

RECEPTIONIST

Uh huh,... Uh huh.. Okay.. Thanks.

The receptionist hangs up the receiver and turns to Nick.

RECEPTIONIST

I'm sorry, but Ron is unavailable. He asks that you come back in nine months.

Nick looks quizzically.

NICK

Nine months?

RECEPTIONIST

Yes, he says he'll be busy 'til then.

NICK

Is he pregnant?

INT. ROCK BOX SALES OFFICE - DAY

• • •

Ed, Frank, Bob, and Nick are all in the office doing paperwork or talking on the phone. Nick walks over to Bob and speaks to him in a low tone of voice.

NICK

What goes on at these Sales Meetings?

BOB

Basically, Edward gets up and chews us new ass holes.

NICK

Really?

BOB

Edward knows nothing of psychology. He thinks you motivate by threat. Expect the worst.

INT. ROCK BOX CONFERENCE ROOM - DAY

• • •

All the salesmen are seated around the conference table as Edward Moss walks around the room, talking at a louder than normal level. Edward appears agitated. The salesmen all have concerned looks on their faces.

EDWARD

Does everyone in this room understand?

The salesmen all nod affirmatively.

EDWARD

Fine. The change will take place tomorrow morning. Now go out there and sell boxes.

Edward walks to the door and exits.

INT. ROCK BOX HALLWAY FROM CONFERENCE ROOM - DAY

• • •

Edward is walking down the hall from the meeting he just held. He shakes his head and wiggles his shoulders as though relieved that he pulled this meeting off and got out unscathed.

INT. ROCK BOX CONFERENCE ROOM - DAY

All the salesmen appear visibly shaken. Nick leans over toward Bob.

NICK

I understand that part about not doing our share, and possibly losing our jobs. What the hell was that bit about levels? I don't understand.

BOB

Levels are how Rock Box screws salesmen. Their pricing system has a code that designates how much we get paid for anything we sell. A "C" level pays better than an "A" level. An "F" level pays better than a "D". Well, what that bully just told us is that they're changing the structure of the levels. So what was an "F" is now a "D". That means you take a cut in pay. That is, unless you can sell more so you can earn the same as before. Before too long, you'll learn to despise him.

Nick's face turns long as he faces the reality.

INT. ROCK BOX LOBBY - DAY

A man walks in and approaches the receptionist.

MAN

Good morning, I'm here to see Teddy.

The receptionist looks puzzled.

RECEPTIONIST

Teddy? There isn't a Teddy here.

MAN

Teddy Moss.

RECEPTIONIST

Oh, Edward Moss. Yes. Is he expecting you?

MAN

Yes he is. He's my neighbor, and I asked him if I could have some cardboard sheets for my daughter to decorate for a school play. He told me I could come by today.

RECEPTIONIST

I'll tell him you're here.

The receptionist picks up the phone and keys in.

RECEPTIONIST

Edward, your neighbor is here.

. . .

INT. ROCK BOX LOBBY - DAY

Edward enters the lobby.

MAN

(Enthusiastically)

Hi, Teddy. Is this a good time to pick up the sheets?

EDWARD

Yes, just fine. I've got someone bringing them out shortly.

Edward walks over to the man and shakes his hand. Edward leans closer to the man and whispers out of hearing range of the receptionist.

EDWARD

In the business world, I'm known as Edward.

INT. OFFICE LOBBY - DAY

Nick's business card is returned to him, as he stands at the receptionists desk.

RECEPTIONIST

Mr. Delage isn't interested.

Nick takes his card dejectedly, and turns to leave.

NICK

Thanks.

INT. OFFICE LOBBY - DAY

Nick is standing at the receptionist desk. The receptionist hands Nick his business card back and shakes her head negatively.

INT. ROCK BOX SALES OFFICE - DAY

• • •

Nick walks into the sales office and finds Bob sitting at his desk.

NICK

How's it going?

BOB

Good. How's the rookie doing?

NICK

Not so hot.

BOB

What? Spoken by the very man who told me, and quite recently, "How hard can it be?"

NICK

Okay. Okay. So I was a little naive.

BOB

You'll do fine. You're just in a temporary lull, that's all. It happens to all of us.

NICK

Thanks for trying to cheer me up.

BOB

I do know something that could cheer you up.

NICK

What, a winning lottery ticket?

BOB

No. Not that good. Take a walk down to the accountant's office and see what I mean.

NICK

Didn't he quit a few weeks ago?

BOB

Yes, he did. His successor is in and it's not a him. In fact, she's not like any she I've ever seen before.

NICK

Are you interested in her?

BOB

Hell, no. I'm an overweight and over-the- hill plain guy. She wouldn't look twice at me. But you, you'd be right up her alley.

NICK

Oh, and you know this by looking at her? For all you know, she could be married.

BOB

No rings. I already looked.

NICK

Maybe a boyfriend?

BOB

Making excuses again? Allowing yourself an out?

NICK

Okay. Okay. I'll take a walk down there.

INT. DOORWAY OF ACCOUNTANT'S OFFICE - DAY

Nick walks to the threshold of the office. He looks in as the new accountant looks up from her work. Their eyes meet. She is beautiful. He looks at her for what seems an excessive amount of time without either of them speaking. She stares back at him. Finally, Nick enters the office and extends his hand.

NICK

Hi. My name is Nick. I'm a salesman here. Well, only for a few months now.

BONNIE

Hi, I'm Bonnie. This is my second day.

Their eyes remain locked on each other. There appears to be an attraction at work, and they both know it.

NICK

Have you been an accountant long?

BONNIE

Since I got out of school.

NICK

So the job's a natural fit?

BONNIE

Not really. There's so many things that are different from what I've known or done that I may have bitten off more than I can chew. I'm starting to worry.

Nick and Bonnie's eyes are still locked on to each other. Nick's expression shows a sign of surprise that Bonnie is being so candid to a total stranger.

NICK

Don't worry. That's just your mind trying to defeat you. I go through it all the time.

Nick chuckles, trying to make light of Bonnie's concerns.

NICK

Well, I just wanted to welcome you and wish you luck.

BONNIE

Thanks so much. It was really nice of you.

Nick and Bonnie's gaze continues. They reluctantly break off as Nick leaves her office. Edward Moss sees Nick leaving Bonnie's office. His expression is one of suspicion.

INT. OFFICE - DAY

Nick walks up to a receptionist, reaches into his pocket for a business card. He hands the business card to the receptionist.

NICK

Is it possible to see the person that
purchases boxes for your company?

RECEPTIONIST

I'm sorry, the purchasing agent doesn't see anyone without an appointment.

NICK That's fine, could I please have his or her name so that I can call and make an appointment?

RECEPTIONIST

I'm sorry, we're not allowed to give out any names.

The receptionist looks very matter-of-factly as she speaks the words. Nick's expression turns to puzzlement, considering the "catch 22" he has just encountered. He reluctantly shrugs his shoulders, nods acknowledgment, turns around, and heads for the front door. He suddenly turns around again and walks up to the receptionist.

NICK

Would it be possible to use your men's room?

RECEPTIONIST

I'm sorry, our rest rooms facilities are for employees only.

NICK

Could you give me a job quick?

The receptionist shakes her head no, with a hint of a smile, acknowledges Nick's attempt at humor. Nick shrugs his shoulders again, and turns around once again and heads for the door.

EXT. OFFICE BUILDING - DAY

Nick walks down the walkway hurriedly. He's now hunched over slightly, in apparent discomfort for his need to relieve himself. He approaches his car, which is in the company's parking lot. Still hunched over, he inserts his key into the door lock. His eyes dart left and right, desperately scanning the parking lot. His eyes spot an area of bushes not far from his car. Nick quickly makes his way to the bushes, still hunched uncomfortably. He unzips his fly and proceeds to relieve himself into the bushes. A sigh of relief is heard, as he slowly starts to straighten up progressively.

INT. NICK'S CAR - DAY

Nick pulls out of the parking space in reverse. He puts the transmission in forward and drives to the exit gate of the parking lot. He looks up at the gate to see a sign that reads: Warning. Parking lot is monitored 24 hours a day by video surveillance. Nick's expression turns to embarrassment as he gulps. He stops for a moment, then pulls out of the parking lot.

INT. OFFICE RECEPTION AREA - DAY

Nick walks up to the reception desk. The counter has easel stands with advertisement of the company's product lines. The ads are all products for black people. Afro sheen products, shaving products and miscellaneous toiletries.

NICK

Would it be possible to see the person that purchases boxes for your company?

RECEPTIONIST

I'll see if he's free. That would be the president of the company, William Price.

NICK
(Quizzically)

The president?

RECEPTIONIST

Yes. This is a small company and we all wear many hats.

The receptionist presses a button on the console and makes a connection.

RECEPTIONIST

Mr. Price, I have a man here, Mr. Williams, from Rock Box asking to see you? (Pause). Sure. I'll tell him. Thank you.

The receptionist looks at Nick.

RECEPTIONIST

William Price will be right out to see you.

A moment later, a tall black man enters the lobby. The man looks at Nick with a look of surprise. He then extends his hand to shake Nick's.

MR. PRICE

Billy Price.

NICK

Nick Williams, pleased to meet you.

MR. PRICE

Same here. When my receptionist told me your name, I thought you might be a brother.

Nick looks puzzled by the comment not knowing how to answer.

MR. PRICE

I started this business four years ago, from the ground up. Lotta hard work. Long hours. SBA minority loan, finding a good location, finding good people, not a cake walk.

NICK

I'm sure. I bet you're proud of your efforts.

MR. PRICE

I am. But I'm disappointed in the lack or shortage of brothers in business. Can you tell me why I've never met a black box salesman?

NICK

I don't really know. I've only been selling a short time now.

MR. PRICE

This is some jive shit man. I needs to do business with some brothers.

Billy Price leans into Nick speaking to him almost nose to nose.

NICK

I guess you don't want to buy from me?

Billy Price shakes his head back and forth. A very frustrating No.

INT. OFFICE LOBBY - DAY

Nick stands at a receptionist's desk. The receptionist hands Nick's business card back to him. Nick's expression starts to turn to disappointment.

RECEPTIONIST

Mr. Vega will see you now.

A happy grin comes on Nick's face.

RECEPTIONIST

Mr. Vega's office is down the corridor. Last door on the right.

INT. MR. VEGA'S OFFICE - DAY

Nick arrives at Vince Vega's open office door and knocks. Vince is sitting at his desk, head propped against his open hand, flipping through a magazine, looking totally bored. He speaks without looking up.

VINCE

What the fuck do you want?

NICK

My name is Nick. I sell boxes. Want to buy some?

VINCE

Maybe.

Vince finally looks up from his magazine for the first time. Nick and Vince converse. While they talk, Vince keeps returning to his magazine, turning pages all the while.

NICK (V.O.)

This might not have been my best opening line to a new prospect, but I figured, Vince wasn't exactly going out of his way to make me feel comfortable either. The way I was looking at it, either he was having fun with me or he was a prick looking to bust someone's balls. Not knowing which, I clowned with him until I learned that he was having fun with me.

VINCE

Want a drink?

NICK

Now?

VINCE

Of course now.

Vince gets up and closes his office door. He returns to his chair and spins his chair around to the file cabinet behind it. He pulls open a drawer and takes out a half filled bottle of Absolut Vodka and two glasses.

NICK

They let you drink at work?

VINCE

Who's to say anything? I'm the manager. Besides, I drink vodka. They can't smell it on me.

Vince proceeds to pour two glasses of vodka. He hands one to Nick.

VINCE

Salud.

As he toasts Nick's glass, a mischievous grin appears on Nick's face.

NICK

Thanks. After a day like mine, I could really use this.

VINCE

That bad?

• • •

Vince puts his feet up on his desk and reclines back in his chair.

NICK

This business is a bitch. People won't see you, so you can't sell to them. On top of that, I've got a boss who's riding my ass like a rented mule because I'm not selling enough.

VINCE

Why'd you get into it?

NICK

I need to help my grandmother out. I thought I could make a lot of money fast.

VINCE

There's no easy way in life.

NICK

I guess so.

VINCE

Guess so? You ought to know so! Do you have any Italian blood in you?

NICK

Yeah. On my mom's side.

VINCE

I'm all Italian. Your intelligence comes from your Italian blood.

(CONTINUED)

(MORE)

VINCE (CONT'D)

All those other nationalities blood mixed in screws everything up. That's where those naive notions of how easy life was going to be come from. I'm one hundred percent Italian. No watered down inferior shit here.

Vince looks at Nick intently to see if Nick understands. He continues.

VINCE

I like you, kid, and I'm rarely wrong about first impressions. Listen, I buy over a million dollars in boxes a year. I've been buying from one company all along, but they've been fucking me.

Vince stops mid-sentence to make his point. He shakes his finger in the air to emphasize his view.

VINCE

My business is up for grabs. A smart businessman wouldn't tell you this, because you'd smell blood, and take advantage of me. But, like I said, I like you, and I trust you. I'd like to help both you and your grandmother out. I'll fax you a list of items I use. Quote them, and we'll go from there.

. . .

Nick's face illuminates at the turn of events.

NICK

I won't let you down. Thanks for the opportunity.

Nick rises from his seat and moves toward Vince to shake his hand.

VINCE

Where the fuck do you think you're going? You haven't finished your drink yet. Besides, I want to hear more about your family in Italy.

Nick smiles, and returns to his seat. He picks up his glass of vodka.

NICK

My grandfather was from Palermo. He grew up in ..

NICK (V.O.)

This is how all sales calls should go. Unfortunately, this is the exception. Vince and I hit it off incredibly well. I don't know how much the Italian blood part helped my cause, but it helped. We quoted his items and came in close enough to the supplier he hated, that he gave me all his business. This was a major turning point for me. Vince, in essence, became a customer for life at that instant. Sometimes this business is so hard, and then it's so easy, as in Vince's case. Just so you don't get too headstrong and almighty, there are always calls like this one, that'll reestablish your feet on the ground.

INT. PROSPECT'S OFFICE - DAY

Nick is seated in front of an unkempt looking individual. The man is picking his nose with his right hand. He's doing it in intervals, as if to be less noticeable.

NICK

Our capabilities in corrugated are almost limitless. We have three color capacity. We can automatically glue almost any size box. Do you have a wide range of sizes?

MAN

No. Almost all my cartons are small.

The man's right finger goes back to his nostril as he finishes the sentence.

NICK

Well, I would like an opportunity to quote your cartons when it might be appropriate.

MAN

Okay. I'm sure I'll call you someday.

He finishes his sentence and rises from his chair. He walks over to Nick and extends his right hand for a handshake. Nick looks down at the man's hand and hesitates, thinking back only moments ago at what he was doing with his finger. Nick gulps, then reaches his hand out to complete this shake. Nick's expression is of resignation.

EXT. OFFICE BUILDING - DAY

Nick is walking out to his car, wiping his right hand on the thigh of his trousers. Sighs of disgust are heard.

INT. ROCK BOX OFFICE - DAY

Nick walks into Bonnie's Office. Their eyes lock once again.

NICK

How's it going?

BONNIE

Okay I guess. I'm still here.

NICK

You have doubts?

BONNIE

This job is tough and I still don't feel like I've figured it all out.

NICK

Is the job that difficult or are you always this insecure at new challenges?

BONNIE

I think a little of both.

NICK

You've just summed up my situation in my job. A little of both.

The two's eyes are locked on each other and a strong connection is apparent.

NICK

Would you like to go out?

Bonnie doesn't lose a second responding.

BONNIE

Sure.

NICK

Are you free Saturday?

BONNIE

Yeah.

NICK

How about a picnic down by the water? Do you like Beavertail Point?

BONNIE

I love Beavertail. I haven't been there in years. I love all the little shops in the center of town, too.

NICK

Great. We'll do the shops in the afternoon and then picnic by the water, watching the sunset.

BONNIE

That sounds great.

NICK

What time will you be ready?

BONNIE

Noon would be OK. I'll give you a map to my apartment.

INT. NICKS CAR - DAY

. . .

Bonnie and Nick pull up to a parking spot near the shops.

EXT. SHOPPING DISTRICT - DAY

Nick and Bonnie walk along the street, looking in the windows of the stores.

NICK

Do people really buy things in stores like these or do they just kick tires, wasting salespeople's time asking stupid questions about the out-of-the ordinary things they sell?

BONNIE

You're really sensitive about salespeople, aren't you?

NICK

I've never thought about it before, but I guess it just seeps in when you do it yourself.

BONNIE

Do you like your work?

NICK

I'm not sure yet. Edward keeps me from having fun. If it wasn't for him, my answer would be yes. I haven't been there long enough to know a lot about him. What I have heard isn't good.

BONNIE

How do you mean?

NICK

Well, for one, he cares for no one but himself. My info comes from many sources, not just my opinion. Everyone who'll talk candidly about him is in agreement. He seems to have a problem with seeing salesmen make money. He screws with the compensation system all the time, always to his benefit, and to the salesman's disadvantage. His annual bonus is based on how much he keeps from us. This isn't the way the company explains it, but that's the way it is. Edward is an evil man. He reminds me of my father. He was a sick fuck, too.

Bonnie looks at Nick, puzzled by his statement. As Nick finishes speaking, a car door opens at the curb. An attractive lady in a short skirt steps out of a car, exhibiting a beautiful pair of legs. Nick's gaze goes directly to her legs, momentarily losing his concentration. This doesn't go unnoticed by Bonnie.

NICK
(Continues)

Enough about my battles. How's things with you? Do you like your job?

BONNIE

I think so. I only wish I could feel confident.

NICK

You talk about confidence or the lack of it a lot. Have you always been that way?

Bonnie looks at Nick with a look of hesitant sincerity.

BONNIE

It goes back a long way.

EXT. ROCKY SHORE - DAY

Nick and Bonnie are sitting on a blanket. A picnic basket is opened. A bottle of wine is visible as are dinner plates, silverware and cloth napkins.

BONNIE

I grew up as the only girl in an all male family. I have five brothers and a father. My mother died in childbirth. Mine.

Bonnie looks away as she speaks.

BONNIE

Growing up with all boys isn't an enjoyable experience. Although my brothers all looked out for me, we never really related. As for my father, forget it. No clue. The only way I would have ever connected would have been by joining peewee football, hockey, and softball. My dad's a nice guy, if you're a guy. I never could live up to his expectations, because his expectations were male oriented. As I was growing, I noticed it more. When the division became most apparent, in my early teens, which, incidentally, is the time a girl needs a mother most, he wasn't there. Just because he didn't know he was supposed to be there. And I also wondered if he held me responsible for my mother's death because it was my birth that led to her death. So you asked earlier about my feelings of inadequacy. Well. Now you know.

Nick looks at Bonnie with profound sympathy. He takes her hand in his. She is touched by his sensitivity. The sunlight silhouettes their profiles. Their eyes meet again with the same intensity they experience in the office.

• • •

INT. ROCK BOX - DAY

Nick is walking down the hall when Edward's secretary, Ann, stops him in the hall.

ANN

Nick, could I please see you in the conference room?

NICK

Sure, be right there.

INT. CONFERENCE ROOM - DAY

Nick and Ann are seated at the conference table.

ANN

First, I want to say I'm embarrassed about what I'm going to say. I wish that certain people in here would mind their own business. I've been asked to speak to you about the new girl in accounting, Bonnie. The saying goes, "Don't shit where you eat." I personally don't care what people do in their own time, but certain people here make it their business. So there, I've told you. I've done my job.

Ann looks at Nick somewhat relieved at getting it over with. Nick looks very surprised, and embarrassed.

NICK

Edward?

ANN

I can't say. You can draw your own conclusions.

Ann smiles at Nick, confirming his guess.

NICK

What if she hit on me? What if she is the aggressor?

ANN

Nothing you can do about that, I guess.

INT. CORRIDOR - DAY

Nick walks down the corridor. He stops at Bonnie's doorway. Bonnie looks up from her work to see Nick and their eyes lock on to each other.

NICK

Hi.

BONNIE

Hi.

NICK

I had a nice time Saturday.

BONNIE

So did I. It was a wonderful day.

NICK

Would you like to go out for a drink after work?

BONNIE

Sure. Where? When?

NICK

Well, I have to run out now to visit a turkey-stuffing company with a display proposal. They're in the city. Do you want to meet at Barney's?

BONNIE

Sure, that's fine. Five- thirty?

NICK

Yeah. That's Okay. I should have my call finished by then.

Bonnie pushes her chair away from her desk to reach her file cabinet behind her. Nick's eyes go to Bonnie's legs, as her long, black stockinged legs extend outward as she reaches backward. She notices Nick's gaze. She pulls a folder out of the cabinet, resumes a normal seated posture in her chair, and creeps it back to her desk, all the while noticing Nick's stare.

BONNIE

Want to see something?

Bonnie pushes her chair slightly away from her desk. She grabs the hem of her skirt and pulls it up her leg.

BONNIE

I couldn't help but notice your visually oriented nature.

Bonnie stops pulling up her skirt at the top of her lace topped stockings. Nick continues to stare in stunned silence. He forms an "O" with his lips and exhales as he stares at Bonnie.

NICK

Now you've done it. Now, I've gotta go home tonight and jerk off.

Bonnie smiles at his response as she pulls her skirt back down.

NICK

In fact, why should I wait until tonight?

Nick walks away from Bonnie's doorway.

INT. BONNIE'S OFFICE - DAY

. . .

Bonnie looks up from her work to see Nick return to her doorway, smiling. Nick leans against the door jamb, crosses his arms and exhibits an ever increasing grin.

NICK

Thanks, It was great!

Bonnie looks confused at his remark.

BONNIE

What?

NICK

Thanks.

BONNIE

For What?

. . .

Bonnie still looks puzzled. Slowly her expression starts to change as she starts to understand his remarks.

BONNIE

You didn't?

NICK

Sure did. It was convenient having the men's room next to your office.

Bonnie repeats her words again, almost disbelievingly.

BONNIE

You didn't?

NICK

You're right. I didn't. I was just testing your sense of humor. I love discovering new things about you.

BONNIE

Get out of here.

Bonnie shakes her head and smiles as she returns to her paperwork.

NICK

Still see you at Barney's at five thirty?

Bonnie looks hesitantly, then smiles.

BONNIE

Of course.

INT. CUSTOMER'S OFFICE - DAY

• • •

Nick has a display set up in the purchaser's office. The display is a supermarket type that stands upright. There are many shelves and compartments to hold bags of turkey stuffing mix.

NICK

What do you think?

MR. SIMPSON

I like it a lot. Don't you think that the shelves and compartments should be pitched backward a little more?

NICK

I think that's a personal preference. We can make it any way you want. Tell me what you want and I'll get you another sample.

MR. SIMPSON

I can't wait. This product is expected in markets in a few weeks. Skip the sample. I don't have the time. Just redesign the upper part of the display to tilt back two or three more degrees. I think that's all it needs. I'll give you an order to take with you to get this going.

NICK

OK. Two or three degrees? Or should we go five?

MR. SIMPSON

That'll do it. Go for five.

EXT. PARKING LOT - DAY

Nick is putting the display into the back seat of his car.

NICK (V.O.)

Things are finally starting to click. Someone once told me "If you throw enough shit at the wall, some of its got to stick."

• • •

Nick looks at his wristwatch to see its almost four p.m.

NICK (V.O.)

I've still got time to make one more cold call before I meet up with Bonnie. This day's been going my way so far. Who knows? Maybe my next new account is only a sales call away.

INT. PROSPECT'S OFFICE - DAY

Nick is seated across from a prospective buyer. Nick's expression is of frustration laced with boredom. The person he's visiting is talking incessantly and laughing obnoxiously at his own intentionally placed jokes.

NICK

So, you think we may be able to help you?

BUYER

Yeah, with a personal loan. Hah, hah, hah, hah. You asked so I told you. Hah, hah, hah.

NICK (V.O.)

Of course, there's no way to predict the dead ends in the road. Even good, lucky days must end. I curse my decision to stop here. I won't be back.

BUYER

So, you have any free samples? Hah, hah, hah.

EXT. BARNEY'S RESTAURANT - DAY

Nick's car pulls into a parking space in front of Barney's.

INT. BARNEY'S RESTAURANT - DAY

Nick and Bonnie are seated in a booth.

BONNIE

How'd things go at the turkey farm?

NICK

It isn't a farm. It's a stuffing company. It went fine. He placed an order ten thousand displays.

BONNIE

Congratulations.

Bonnie toasts Nick's glass, smiling at him proudly.

NICK

Thanks.

BONNIE

You've been doing pretty well lately. That is, until you pulled that stunt this afternoon.

• • •

Bonnie shakes her head, still in disbelief, but smiles amusedly.

BONNIE

I generate the sales reports, so I can't help but notice. I'm really proud of you. For someone who started recently, you've done yourself proud.

Nick blushes at the adulation. Bonnie looks at him with admiration.

BONNIE

It's getting real easy for you, right?

NICK

Not really. For every good thing that happens, like the turkey stuffing, there's the dead end, like the last guy I visited today. He wasn't looking for a new box supplier. He was looking for a new ear to listen to his dumbass jokes. Hah, Hah, Hah. Shit, I can't get the sound of that hyena's laughter out of my head. Bad choice stopping there.

BONNIE

That bad?

NICK

That bad. Enough about my day. How'd yours go?

BONNIE

I'm catching on. It's a never ending learning process. I'm feeling more confident.

She smiles. Nick reaches out to touch her hand.

NICK

I had the strangest meeting with Ann today. She pulled me aside and warned me about fraternization. Specifically about you.

. . .

Bonnie's eyes open wide at the revelation.

BONNIE

They have that rule?

NICK

I think it's a bunch of bullshit.

BONNIE

I can't take any chances. I need my job.

NICK

No one's going to know. We can keep it under wraps.

BONNIE

You know how long secrets are kept? We can't keep this from people. Nick, you don't know how long I was on unemployment. I can't risk being there again. It's really tough out there. Maybe we should cool it.

NICK

Why? We get along so great. We can't give this up.

BONNIE

We have to. There's no other choice. Besides, it wouldn't work out between us.

NICK

Please explain.

BONNIE

I don't know about you, but I've been in many relationships in my life. They just don't work out.

NICK

Bad relationships don't.

BONNIE

But, they don't start out that way. I mean, most of the time you don't know they're bad until they end. I've experienced a lot of ends.

Nick looks frustrated.

NICK

Oh, and you know this is another bad one?

(Sarcastically)
BONNIE

No, I don't, but they all look great at the outset. It's an exercise in futility.

NICK

Look, I've had bumps in my life too, but I can't give up hope. We can work through it.

BONNIE

Can't we just be friends?

NICK

Okay. Okay. Have it your way. Can we still get together like this once in a while?

BONNIE

Sure. No harm in this. We're just friends. Besides, you still have a girlfriend, don't you?

Nick shrugs his shoulders, yet nods his head affirmatively.

NICK

The relationship is awful, has been for a long time. We have nothing in common. Besides, we haven't seen much of each other lately.

BONNIE

Why do you still go with Kathy? Her name is Kathy?

NICK

Yeah. Kathy.

BONNIE

Why do you stay with her?

Bonnie appears to be helping Nick get down to his feelings on the subject.

BONNIE

Don't tell me it's for the sex only?

Nick shrugs his shoulders ashamedly.

NICK

Maybe it is. I haven't tried to analyze it.

BONNIE

Men!

INT. CUSTOMER'S OFFICE - DAY

Nick is seated in a customer's office. The customer is a heavily overweight man in his sixties. Both are holding copies of a quotation.

DAVE

These prices look very competitive. We can do business.

NICK

That's great.

DAVE

Could we go out to lunch sometime?

NICK

Of course. Why, we could go today if you're free. It's eleven thirty now.

DAVE

Sure. But I have a stop I need to make. Is it OK?

NICK

Of course.

EXT. NICK'S CAR - DAY

Nick is driving, with Dave as a passenger. Dave has a stack of bank books in his hands.

DAVE

You sure this isn't a problem for you to stop at the bank?

NICK

No, it's fine.

EXT. CITY ROAD - DAY

Nick pulls into the bank parking lot. Dave struggles to get out of the car, because of his size, and goes into the bank.

EXT. BANK PARKING LOT - DAY

Dave walks out of the bank and gets into Nick's car.

INT. NICK'S CAR - DAY

Nick and Dave are driving out of the bank parking lot.

DAVE

Would you mind making one more stop?

NICK

No, not at all.

DAVE

I've got to pick up a pair of shoes at the cobbler's.

NICK

No problem.

EXT. CITY ROAD - DAY

Nick pulls up to the cobbler shop. Dave struggles out of the car again and enters the cobbler's shop.

• • •

INT. CITY ROAD - DAY

Dave comes out of the cobbler shop with a pair of shoes in his hand.

INT. NICK'S CAR - DAY

Dave enters the car and closes the door. He sets the pair of shoes in his lap.

DAVE

I'm hungry. Are you?

NICK

Sure am. Where to?

DAVE

Lizzie's on Broadway. Okay?

NICK

Sure.

INT. LIZZIE'S RESTAURANT - DAY

Dave and Nick are sitting at a table. A waiter approaches.

WAITER

Would you gentlemen like a cocktail?

DAVE

I'll have a Bloody Mary.

NICK

That sounds fine. Make it two.

The waiter takes the order and walks away.

DAVE

Do you read porn magazines?

NICK

Not regularly. I do see an occasional issue.

DAVE

I love naked women. I love looking at them.

NICK

Who doesn't?

DAVE

I really love them. I can't get enough of them. I'm at the newsstand every month. I've got quite a collection.

NICK

What about your wife?

. . .

The waiter interrupts the conversation with the two Bloody Marys.

WAITER

Are you ready to order?

DAVE

No, not yet. We'll let you know.

WAITER

Fine.

The waiter walks away. Dave resumes the conversation.

DAVE

Of course, she doesn't know. I keep them in boxes in my basement. She never looks down there.

• • •

Dave take a drink from his Bloody Mary. He raises his hand to hail the waiter. The waiter sees him and returns.

WAITER

Yes.

DAVE

Could I have more Tabasco sauce in this drink?

WAITER

Right away.

The waiter takes the drink with him. Dave resumes the conversation.

DAVE

My wife thinks the basement is a man's thing, so no problem.

• • •

The waiter returns with the drink.

WAITER

Would you like to order?

DAVE

No, not yet.

The waiter nods, then walks away. Dave takes a sip of his Bloody Mary. Dave raises his hand to hail the waiter once again. The waiter sees him and returns to their table.

WAITER

Yes.

DAVE

Could I please have more Worcestershire sauce in this drink?

WAITER

Sure. Be right back.

The waiter takes the drink and returns to the bar. Dave continues speaking.

DAVE

Do you have any porn magazines?

NICK

I might have a few issues.

Dave chuckles in a mischievous way.

DAVE

Well, if you ever get sick of them, you know who you can give them to.

• • •

The waiter returns with Dave's drink. The waiter walks away. Dave take a sip. He contemplates swallowing, then raises his hand again. The waiter sees him from across the room. The waiter walks back to Dave, trying to hide his disgust.

WAITER

Yes.

DAVE

Could you please put some more horseradish in this drink?

WAITER

OK.

The waiter takes Dave's drink again and walks back to the bar.

DAVE

Do you think you might have some magazines for me?

(Dave looks devilishly)

NICK

I'm sure I can get you some.

The waiter return this time with the drink and a dish with three lemon slices, as if to anticipate Dave's next request. Dave picks up the drink, and the waiter remains in anticipation of being waved back again.

NICK (V.O.)

Dave became a big customer, no pun intended, so you learn to bite your tongue, rather than bite the hand that feeds you. He's amusing as hell, as long as you don't take him too seriously. Now, all I've got to do is get him some porn magazines to really make him happy.

• • •

INT. ROCK BOX OFFICE - DAY

Nick walks up to Bonnie's doorway. Bonnie looks up at Nick. Their eyes meet and the attraction can easily be seen.

NICK

How've you been?

BONNIE

OK. Been busy.

NICK

Are you free for a drink after work?

Bonnie raises her eyebrows in a questioning manner.

BONNIE

Nick, I'd love to, but you know the rules.

NICK

What rules? There aren't any rules. It's only that prick, Edward, micro managing his domain.

Bonnie looks startled at the revelation.

BONNIE

Edward?

NICK

I looked into it. The corporation doesn't have any fraternization rules. It's only Edward making up rules as he goes along.

Bonnie's expression is one of confusion and then understanding. She sits in silence, looking away.

NICK

What's the matter? Are you OK?

BONNIE

I'm not sure. This is all so crazy.

NICK

What is?

Bonnie motions Nick to come closer to her. Bonnie leans toward Nick and whispers to him.

BONNIE

Edward's been hitting on me since I was hired.

Nick is stunned by what he's heard. It only takes moments for him to go from stunned to angered.

NICK

That son of a bitch. (Pause) Have you gone out with him?

BONNIE

Of course not. Not as of yet. He comes on strong, then he backs away. I've been able to hold him off up 'til now, but I'm afraid of what will happen if he really starts pressuring me. I told you that I really need this job.

NICK

How've you been stalling him?

BONNIE

I keep reminding him that he's got a wife and kids, not to mention that I'm probably twenty years younger than him. He just won't give up. Like I don't have enough problems in life without this.

Nick is still visibly upset by this revelation.

NICK

That bastard! First he fucks with our commissions, then he interferes with our lives.

Nick and Bonnie's visual exchange mirrors the hopelessness of their situation.

INT. EDWARD MOSS'S KITCHEN - MORNING

Edward is eating breakfast and reading the morning paper. His wife is cleaning the kitchen.

EDWARD'S WIFE

Teddy, when are you going to plant the flowers?

EDWARD

I'll try to do them this weekend.

EDWARD'S WIFE

This weekend? You've been saying that for weeks now. You should do them after work.

EDWARD

I'm too tired after work. I'll do it this weekend.

EDWARD'S WIFE

You should be playing with your son on weekends. You do remember your son? Your neglected son who needs attention.

EDWARD

He's got friends.

EDWARD'S WIFE

You couldn't be any more useless if you tried. Teddy, you make me crazy.

EDWARD

Well, gotta go. I've got a sales meeting to run this morning. Business is off.

EDWARD'S WIFE

I couldn't care less.

Edward's son, Teddy Jr., runs into the kitchen from the adjacent room.

TEDDY JR.

Dad, can I have my G.I. Joe back?

EDWARD

No! You know you're being punished. Now get ready for school.

TEDDY JR.

No. I won't. I want my G.I. Joe back.

EDWARD

Get lost. I'm going to work.

Edward heads for the rear kitchen door. His son follows him out the door, making a whining sound.

EXT. EDWARD'S DRIVEWAY - MORNING

Edward walks down the driveway. His son is in pursuit. Edward gets into his car and starts it. His son goes to the open passenger window and proceeds to whine.

TEDDY JR.

I want my G.I. Joe now!

EDWARD

Get away from the car. I have to go.

TEDDY JR.

Make me. I'm not letting go.

Teddy Jr. hangs onto the car by draping his arms over the open window of the door.

EDWARD

Get off the car. Now!

Edward puts the car into gear and proceeds to drive down the driveway. Teddy Jr. still hangs on.

TEDDY JR.

I won't get off 'til you give me my G.I. Joe back!

Edward drives the car back and forth on the driveway, trying to get his son to let go.

EDWARD

Get the hell off the car! You're going to make me late.

TEDDY JR.

Give me back my G.I. Joe!

Edward's patience is now lost. His expression turns to anger and frustration. He's now screaming at his son who tenaciously hangs onto the door. Out of sheer desperation, Edward drives his car over toward a bush at the edge of the driveway. He drives the passenger side of the car back and forth along the bush. Teddy Jr.'s body is being dragged through the bush, yet he still holds on. Edward's wife run out the kitchen door. She's screaming as she runs down the driveway.

EDWARD'S WIFE

Let him go! Let him go! You animal!

EDWARD

He won't get off the car.

• • •

Edward now stops the car, mid-bush, as Teddy Jr. still hangs on, trying to clear his face of the branches.

EDWARD'S WIFE

What the hell are you doing? What are the neighbors going to think?

Edwards wife looks down the street toward the neighbor's homes.

EDWARD'S WIFE

You are such an incredible asshole! Back the car up so Teddy can get off.

Edward backs the car up enough to get Teddy Jr. out of the bush. Edward's wife hugs Teddy Jr. as he still hangs on the car.

EDWARD'S WIFE

What's the matter, honey?

TEDDY JR.

Dad won't give me my G.I. Joe back.

EDWARD'S WIFE

It's okay honey. I'll take you to the store after school and you can buy a whole platoon of G.I. Joes on daddy's credit card.

Teddy Jr. immediately loosens his grip on the car door. He hugs his mother.

TEDDY JR.

Thanks, Mom.

Teddy Jr. runs back into the house. Edward's wife looks contemptuously at Edward.

EDWARD'S WIFE

Asshole.

She turns and follows Teddy Jr. into the house.

EXT. ROCK BOX PARKING LOT - DAY

Edward's car pulls up to the parking spot with his name on it. There are faint scratch marks running the length of the passenger side.

INT. ROCK BOX CONFERENCE ROOM - DAY

All the salesmen are seated around the conference table. Ed, Frank, Bob, and Nick all have the appearance of someone who's been beat on. They're all looking down at the table as Edward continues speaking.

EDWARD

I suspect that some of you won't be here next Monday. I need tough salesmen who can get the job done. I'm greatly disappointed in all of you.

(CONTINUED)

(MORE)

EDWARD (CONT'D)

Because of you, we've got to lay some plant people off. You haven't been bringing enough business in. That's the bottom line.

Bob looks up and interrupts.

BOB

With all due respect, Edward, we're slow because we raised prices higher than our competitors' last year. Our customers have been telling us that for months, yet you said, "It's okay. They don't mean it. They'll pay us more because we're worth it." Well, this shows us. They're not paying us more. A box is a box, and they'll buy them elsewhere if they can get a better deal.

Edward becomes visibly shaken. His face fills with anger.

EDWARD

You don't know what you're talking about. Shut up. Bob, you need to ask yourself right now if you want to be here. I need team players, not malcontents.

BOB

Don't shoot, I'm only the messenger. I'm out there every day, and I'm reporting what I see.

EDWARD

Shut up. You don't know anything. Just listen to me. Forget all this pricing crap. Just get business.

BOB

Pricing doesn't have anything to do with getting business?

(Sarcastically)
EDWARD

That's enough. I don't want to hear another

word from you or you'll be in the unemployment line tomorrow morning.

NICK (V.O.)

Edward had such a way of endearing himself to us all. It was times like this that allowed him to exhibit what he was really made of. He was self centered, self serving, with a total lack of interpersonal skills. Aside from that, he was a great manager. He fancied himself as an expert in selling. I only wish he had to earn his living by selling. I'd get such satisfaction out of watching him starve.

EDWARD

I don't want to hear any more excuses from you disappointing individuals. I only want results or your resignations. Now, get out of here, and earn your keep.

Edward turns away and heads for the door. He leaves the room quickly.

INT. ROCK BOX CORRIDOR - DAY

. . .

Edward enters the hallway from the conference room and quickly retreats toward his office down the hall. He shakes his head and wiggles his shoulders in the same relieved mannerism he exhibits when he pulls off another acting job.

INT. SAMPLE ROOM - DAY

Nick enters the sample room. Steve greets him with a sympathetic look.

STEVE

I just heard about your ass chewing.

NICK

Good news sure travels fast.

STEVE

We didn't have to try too hard. Edward's loud voice traveled down the hall.

NICK

Yeah. He was riled up. Bob really crawled up his ass, which fueled the situation. He threatened to fire us all.

STEVE

Don't consider that a blind threat.

NICK

Why?

STEVE

He's got a reputation for firing rookies.

NICK

He does?

STEVE

Uh huh.

NICK

Why didn't anyone tell me about that?

STEVE

We didn't want to worry you.

NICK

Who's we?

STEVE

Bob and I. We talked about it when you got hired. Bob felt that you'd make it, so there wasn't any point in worrying you.

NICK

How many rookies has Edward fired?

STEVE

Too many. One every year and a half. But that's only been over the past ten years.

NICK
(Sarcastically)

Oh. I feel better already.
That average isn't so bad.

STEVE

He won't fire you. You're the best of the whole lot. You've opened more large accounts than anyone, rookie or veteran.

NICK

You think so?

STEVE

I know so.

The sample room door opens and Bob enters.

STEVE

Hey Bob, hasn't Nick performed beyond his predecessors?

Bob looks at Nick as he speaks.

BOB

You sure have. You don't have to worry about being fired.

NICK

You're that sure?

BOB

Very sure! I'll explain why. You know I was out at corporate last week for the training seminar.

NICK

Yeah?

BOB

Well, I had the opportunity to spend some time with Edward's boss. We had dinner after the seminar. It seems that Edward has taken credit for some of the new accounts you opened.

Nick looks shocked at the revelation.

NICK

He what?

BOB

He only took credit for three of them. It just happened to be the three largest.

NICK

What's he trying to prove?

BOB

What he's trying to prove is simple. You get a reduced rate of commission on those accounts, and he reaps a substantial bonus at year end. That's his cut for helping you land those accounts.

NICK

He had nothing to do with my getting those accounts. How can he do this?

BOB

Easy. He's always done it. As long as I've known him.

(CONTINUED)

(MORE)

BOB(CONT'D)

His boss doesn't question him, and his boss won't be discussing particulars with you, even if he has the occasion to meet you. It's easy stealing.

Nick absorbs his words with painful understanding.

NICK

That unethical, thieving, lowlife piece of shit.

Bob raises his finger in the air as if to make a point.

BOB

Rich piece of shit. I hope he dies before me so I can piss on his grave.

INT. ROCK BOX CORRIDOR. - DAY

• • •

Nick walks down the hall dejectedly. He stops at the doorway of the customer service department. He draws the manager's attention.

NICK

John, could you please take a minute and look something up for me?

JOHN

A minute? You think I have a minute? I got in at seven o'clock this morning to get a jump on the day. I still had work piled up on me from when I returned from vacation two weeks ago. I had orders to process that are already late. Do you think anyone would have done my work when I was out? Of course not. No one cares. Everyone is looking out for themselves.

(CONTINUED)

(MORE)

JOHN(CONT'D)

I used to help people when they were out. It's only common courtesy. Common courtesy doesn't mean squat anymore. I had to go to the dentist Monday morning. Do you think someone would have at least taken my calls while I was out? Fuck no! They took messages. I'm still returning calls from Monday. To add insult to injury, Edward gave me a project to work on. Margin improvement bullshit. I'll give him margin improvement, right up his butt. He thinks that if he piles shit on me, I'll work harder. I'll show that prick. I'm going to let his project back up like a clogged toilet. The last time he gave me a big project to work on, I busted my hump to finish it when he wanted. You know what I got? I had my stroke. Do you think he gave a shit? No. That waste of human life didn't call, send me a card or anything. Can you believe that? So he can kiss my ass if he thinks I'm gonna jump hoops for him now. Do you know what else I'm working on?

NICK

It's okay. I get the picture. Sorry to bother you.

• • •

Nick turns away and heads down the hall.

NICK (V.O.)

I don't think it occurred to John that he spent one and a half minutes explaining to me why he couldn't help me for a minute.

(CONTINUED)

(MORE)

NICK (CONT'D)

I've discovered that it's easier to sell boxes than to get assistance from our own office. Bob was right again. Just when I'm finally feeling good about myself, Edward has to steal my thunder. Damn my luck!

Nick walks up to Bonnie's doorway. He looks at her with sadness. Bonnie looks up at him. She chooses not to engage him in the eye lock they normally share. She looks back down at her desk and returns to work. Nick turns away and continues down the corridor.

NICK (V.O.)

My boss is screwing me, trying to screw my love interest, and she's trying to avoid me. Could things get any more fucked up than they are? You bet they can.

EXT. PORN SHOP PARKING LOT - DAY

Nick drives his car off the road into the parking lot of a porn shop. He gets out of the car and heads for the door.

NICK (V.O.)

My customer, Dave, made such a fuss about skin magazines that I figured it would probably be in my best interest to pick him up a few.

INT. PORN SHOP - DAY

• • •

Nick is picking up various issues. They're all in plastic wrap.

NICK (V.O.)

They put all these magazines in plastic wrap because the girls on the cover always look better than the girls on the inside. The girls on the inside are chicks you wouldn't want to meet, unless, of course, you are Dave.

EXT. PORN SHOP - DAY

Nick walks out of the shop with a paper bag under his arm. He walks over to his car, reaching in his pocket for his keys. He fumbles, searching his pants and jacket pockets. Not finding the keys, he looks in the car and sees them in the ignition. Nick stomps the ground, looks at the car, then at the porn shop.

NICK

Shit!

• • •

Nick walks over to a nearby pay phone and dials.

FEMALE VOICE (V.O.)

Rock Box, good afternoon.

NICK

Hi, Sue, It's Nick. Can I speak to Ann?

FEMALE VOICE (V.O.)

Hold on. I think she's in with Edward.

ANN (V.O.)

Hi, Nick. What can I do for you?

NICK

Well, I locked myself out of the car. Could you please check and see if there's a spare set of keys for my car?

ANN (V.O.)

Yes. I have spare keys for all the cars.

NICK

Could someone bring them to me?

ANN (V.O.)

Sure. Where are you?

Nick looks at the porn shop, and then at his car. He scans the surroundings. There are no landmarks other than the phone booth he's using.

NICK

Uh, I'm on the side of the road, uh, half a mile south of the Route 2 and Route 4 Junction. Uh, and there's a telephone booth near my car.

ANN

Any other landmarks?

NICK

Uh, no, only the phone booth. I'll be here waiting.

ANN (V.O.)

Edward is leaving soon for lunch. I'll see if he can bring the keys to you.

NICK

No, don't ask him. Could you please bring them instead?

INT. NICK'S CAR - DAY

Nick is driving down the road with a look of relief on his face. His car phone rings.

NICK

Hello.

SUE (V.O.)

Hi, Nick. You have a message from Mr. Simpson at Turkey Stuffing Co. He says it's urgent.

NICK

I'm not far from there. I'll be there in fifteen minutes. Thanks.

INT. MR. SIMPSON'S OFFICE - DAY

Nick and Mr. Simpson are both standing in his office, looking incredulously at the new display that Nick sold him. Turkey stuffing bags are all over the floor because the upper part of the display tilts forward instead of backward.

MR. SIMPSON

I told you, tilt it two or three degrees.

NICK

You changed it to five degrees.

MR. SIMPSON

OK It was five degrees. But not forward. I thought you people are professionals. What kind of asshole would design something like this? All I know is your people are responsible, and I've got ten thousand displays due in supermarkets next week. I suggest you figure something out, and fast.

INT. ROCK BOX OFFICE - DAY

Nick, Steve and the plant manager are looking at the turkey stuffing display. They're all shaking their heads in disbelief.

PLANT MANAGER

We really fucked this one up for you, didn't we?

NICK

Yeah, but also saved the day by getting the replacement committed by this weekend.

PLANT MANAGER

Least we could do. Nothing two shifts of overtime couldn't fix.

Sue, the receptionist, interrupts the meeting.

SUE

Nick, it's a call for you. A retirement center.

NICK

Thanks. Put in at my desk.

Nick excuses himself from the meeting and exits the room.

INT. SALES OFFICE - DAY

. . .

Nick picks up the phone.

NICK

Hello.

VOICE (V.O.)

Is this Nick Williams?

NICK

Yes, I'm Nick.

VOICE (V.O.)

This is Brookwood Retirement Center. I'm afraid your grandmother's not doing well. Her illness has gone on for quite some time now. She's taken a turn for the worse.

NICK

I didn't realize it was so serious. I just saw her last week.

VOICE (V.O.)

Her vital signs are in decline.

NICK

I'll be right over. Thank you. Bye.

Nick hangs up the phone. He takes his sport jacket off the chair and puts it on. The phone rings again.

NICK

Hello.

SUE (V.O.)

Nick. It's Toni from Icy Teas Co. Sounds important.

NICK

Put her through.

Nick hangs up the phone. The phone rings and Nick picks it up.

NICK

Hello.

TONI (V.O.)

Nick, it's Toni. I need to see you right now. The owner and his partners are here and they don't like the way your box is running.

NICK

What's wrong?

TONI (V.O.)

I think it's our machine that's at fault. They're blaming the box. The plant's production is down and their having a shit hemorrhage.

Nicks demeanor turns to resignation.

NICK

I'll be right there.

INT. ICY TEAS PLANT - DAY

Nick and several people are crawling over the machine that puts twenty-four bottles of iced tea into a box. Nick sees something that draws his attention.

NICK

Does this look right?

Nick leans over and points to something at the feed section of the machine.

TONI

No. That isn't normal. Bob. Take a look at this.

Bob the maintenance worker, looks under the machine with Nick and Toni.

BOB

The rail adjuster is
disconnected. I didn't see that before.

Nick looks impatiently at Toni.

NICK

I guess you're all set now.

TONI

I guess so. Could you please stay and watch it run just in case?

NICK
(halfheartedly)
Okay.

INT. ICY TEAS PLANT - DAY

The machine is now running, with case after case of Icy Teas exiting the machine.

NICK

Looks okay to me.

TONI

I think that just about does it. Thanks for responding so quickly. All of us really appreciate it.

NICK

It's okay.

Nick shakes hands with Toni and the rest of the observers and hurriedly leaves the building.

INT. BROOKWOOD RETIREMENT CENTER - DAY

Nick quickly walks up to the receptionist's desk.

NICK

Hi. I'm Nick Williams. Could you tell me how my grandmother is?

The receptionist's expression turns to sadness.

NURSE

I'm very sorry, Mr. Williams, but your grandmother passed away a half hour ago.

Nick stands at the desk numbed by what he's just been told. He doesn't utter a sound, but the look in his damp eyes shows the pain inside.

. . .

EXT. CEMETERY - DAY

A handful of people stand around the casket at the graveside. A priest stands nearby as people walk up to the casket and place flowers on the lid. Nick is the last one to place a flower on the casket. He bows down to kiss the lid. Nick walks over to the priest to thank him for his words. They shake hands and exchange sympathetic expressions. As Nick walks away from the graveside, Bonnie meets up with him and gives him a comforting hug.

NICK

Thanks for coming.

BONNIE

Least I could do.

NICK

Do you have time for coffee?

BONNIE

Sure.

INT. COFFEE SHOP BOOTH - DAY

Nick and Bonnie sit in a booth drinking coffee.

BONNIE

Would I be out of line in asking you where Kathy is?

Nick clasps his hands, looks down and replies.

NICK

We had a fight so she stayed home. Well, I actually told her not to come. She got pissed at the way I was mourning my grandmother's death. To her, the whole world is black and white. My grandmother was old, so she had to go. Everybody has to die sometime, she said. She just didn't get it.

She couldn't accept what she meant to me. My grandmother raised me. If it wasn't for her, I wouldn't be who I am today.

Bonnie looks at Nick puzzled.

BONNIE

I don't understand. What about your parents?

NICK

My parents should never have gotten married, let alone have me. He drank, and she loathed her lot in life. They hated each other, so I was just another burden to their already miserable lives. When I was eleven, they were out one night drinking. My father, drunk as usual, drove off the road. They both died in the crash. Deep down, I think I'll always be angry toward them. They neglected me both in life and in death.

Bonnie touches Nick's hand in a comforting way. Her eyes express deep sympathy. Nick looks at her hand touching his.

NICK

So my grandmother took me in and tried to make up for my parent's shortcomings. She more than made up. She gave me the love and understanding that my parents couldn't. She really loved me. My grandfather died a few years ago, and she lost her house because of the medical bills. She ended up in a retirement home. She was fiercely independent, so she hated life in the home. She tried to hide the fact, but I knew her too well. I took this damn job so that I could help her get her own place again. Now it's too late, and she'll never know what I was planning or how I felt.

Nick chokes up on his words. Bonnie squeezes his hand.

BONNIE

I'm sure she knew.

• • •

Bonnie and Nick look at each other. The deep look in their eyes reminds them both of their visual exchanges in the office. The chemistry is still there. Bonnie's look also tells him she understands him, because they are both very much alike.

EXT. PROSPECT OFFICE - DAY

Nick parks his car in the visitor's parking spot.

INT. PROSPECT'S OFFICE - DAY

Nick is greeted by Dennis Price. Dennis extends his hand.

DENNIS

Hi, Dennis Price. Nice to meet you. Come in.

Dennis motions Nick to his office, which is off of the lobby.

• • •

INT. DENNIS PRICE'S OFFICE - DAY

Dennis points Nick to a chair. Dennis takes the chair behind his desk.

NICK

I was scanning a manufacturer's directory when I found your company name. Do you use a variety of box sizes?

DENNIS

Do I? You bet I do. I buy over a half a million dollars a year.

Nicks eyes light up.

NICK

Are you satisfied with the people you now buy from?

DENNIS

Very happy. They're the best, but I'm always interested in hearing from someone else. Let me tell you about us.

Nick looks at the clock on the wall. It is nine thirty.

INT. DENNIS PRICE'S OFFICE - DAY

Dennis is still talking. Nick is straining to say alert.

DENNIS

So my son tells his wrestling coach, "either give me a chance or I'm quitting."

NICK

Uh, huh.

. . .

Nick looks up at the clock. It is now eleven o'clock.

NICK

Well, I've gotta be going. Can I leave you some literature?

DENNIS

Sure, I'll read it when I get a chance. I'm so damn busy around here. Oh. So the coach, he gets so pissed at my son that he gives him a C minus grade for the quarter. Then, he takes out his anger on my younger son.

NICK

Uh, huh.

Dennis continues talking almost without missing a beat.

NICK (V.O.)

This is the intolerable part of selling. Listening to people ramble on about stuff you could give a shit about, and looking like you care.

EXT. DENNIS PRICE'S COMPANY - DAY

Nick skips down the stairs, heading toward his car with the conviction of a convict making an escape. He shakes his head in disbelief of his predicament for the past two hours.

INT. ROCK BOX OFFICE - DAY

The entire sales force is sitting around the conference table. Edward Moss is speaking in a raised voice.

EDWARD

You gentlemen have to get on the bandwagon. If you don't, I'm leaving you behind. Not one of you has developed a customer for preprinted boxes. You know corporate's position. You have to sell them.

. . .

Bob raises his hand to interrupt.

BOB

Edward, we've been trying, but no one can justify the expense, let alone the massive commitment up front. To expect a customer to commit to a minimum of half a million dollars in one box size is a daunting task.

EDWARD

A daunting task is you in the unemployment office asking for benefits. The president of Rock wants high volume pre-print cartons. He put up a mill to print the paper, and your dead asses are going to sell it. Now, I'm going to ask you again. Do you have any potential customers for preprint?

Edward looks around the table for someone to respond. All the salesmen look down at the table top. Suddenly, Nick looks up.

NICK

I think I can sell Icy Teas preprint boxes.

EDWARD

Are you trying to blow smoke up my ass?

NICK

No. Icy Teas uses two million a year in boxes. I only have to convince them to upgrade the printing from one color to four colors.

EDWARD

Good. Well, get working on it. The rest of you sorry asses better start rethinking as to whether you should be working for this innovative, progressive company. Dead-heads will be replaced.

Edward ends his sentence, turns away quickly, and heads to the door. Edward exits the room. Some of the salesmen follow him out the door. Nick and Bob stay behind. Bob turns to Nick.

BOB

You really think you can talk Icy Teas into it?

NICK

I don't know. I just had to say something to kill the silence. It was too much to take.

BOB

Yeah, But now your ass is on the line. That asshole is going to expect it from you. Rock has invested millions in this mill for pre-print. There's not enough business out there to support it, so they're beating on the salesmen in atonement for their miscalculation. See, it's our fault.

Bob thinks back and shakes his head.

BOB

Threatening me with the unemployment line. That psycho couldn't sell a life jacket to a drowning man. I'm afraid you'll be taking my place as his whipping boy if you don't come across on Icy Teas.

NICK

I'm already on his list. Edward's been picking on me in other ways.

BOB

What other ways?

Nick looks towards the open conference room door. He sees no one there. He leans in toward Bob and speaks in a low tone of voice.

NICK

I've had an interest in Bonnie since she started here. Well, I was warned about fraternization in the office.

BOB

There isn't any fraternization rule here.

NICK

I know that. It's just Edward micro-managing again. The interesting thing is, he's been trying to score her himself.

Bob's expression turns to surprise.

BOB

That son of a bitch. I can't take it anymore. I'm sick of him fucking with our lives. I'd give anything to sabotage his life. I've harbored that fantasy longer than I care to confess. It would be sweet revenge.

NICK

Well, it's a nice thought, but I've got to put that aside and concentrate on selling Icy Teas a million dollars or more in preprinted boxes. In fact, I'm going there now to pitch it.

INT. NICK'S CAR - DAY

Nick is driving his car down a city street. Suddenly, a car pulls out from the right, almost hitting him. Nick veers hard left and manages to avoid the collision. Nick hits the right window down button, pulls alongside the car, and yells.

NICK

Hey, shit head, wake up. Guys like you should take the bus.

As he finishes his sentence, he notices that the driver of the other car is Dennis Price, the prospect he visited yesterday. Dennis recognizes Nick also.

NICK (V.O.)

Another valuable lesson in life. Look before you leap. Thank God, this wasn't anyone I had any hopes of doing business with because I just lost that chance.

INT. EDWARD MOSS'S OFFICE - DAY

Edward is on the phone. A smug look is on his face. The door is closed for privacy.

EDWARD

I think this will be a go.

VOICE (V.O.)

That's terrific, Edward. Did you have this in mind when you landed Icy Teas?

EDWARD

It was in the back of my mind. I was only recently able to pitch the idea to them. I think they'll go for it.

VOICE (V.O.)

I certainly hope you do sell them. If you can close the deal this quarter, you'll receive the bonus that goes with it. The president has offered a

handsome bonus to the general manager who sells preprint. You're the only manager in our region that personally has an account the size of Icy Teas.

So, you're eligible. Who do you have servicing Icy Teas?

EDWARD

I assigned Nick.

VOICE (V.O.)

Don't lose sight of the bigger consideration here. I'm in position to move up to senior vice president soon. That leaves my regional manager position vacant. Your selling preprint to Icy Teas couldn't hurt your chances of advancement.

EDWARD

That's what I'm gunning for.

VOICE (V.O.)

Don't let that deadline slip by. We had a meeting at corporate recently. The topic of extending the deadline came up and it was nixed. So it's only a month away.

EDWARD

I'll sell the program before the deadline.

INT. ICY TEAS - DAY

Nick and Toni are sitting in Toni's Office.

TONI

I was very sorry to hear of your grandmother's passing.

NICK

Thanks. I appreciate it.

TONI

Did she die the day you were here trying to pacify the owners over the problem we were having?

NICK

That was the day. It was almost to the hour.

Toni looks at Nick, trying to read if Nick knew about his grandmother's condition before his visit that day.

TONI

I appreciated your being here that day. I really needed the quick response. But then, that's why I'm doing business with you. Conscientious people are hard to find.

NICK

Thanks for the vote of confidence. It's nice to know you're appreciated.

TONI

Don't mention it. Well, what was this exciting news you wanted to tell me?

Nick reaches in his folio for several pages of literature. He hands it to Toni.

NICK

Our company is now manufacturing pre-printed boxes. The process entails printing the paper before the boxes are made.

The benefit is we can print up to six colors, giving you a box that looks like a photograph. This can't be done any other way.

TONI

What's the catch?

NICK

The catch is the boxes cost a little more, and you need to commit to at least a half million dollars in paper, because they need to print trailer loads of paper for it to make economical sense.

TONI

I'm afraid this couldn't be done.

NICK

Why? You spend enough in boxes a year, don't you?

TONI

Easily. Actually, I buy around two million dollars a year in boxes, split between you and Brand X. If we did go the pre- printed route, I could commit all my boxes to you easily qualifying the half million dollar paper run. My problem is with us. Icy Teas is on shaky ground.

NICK

It is?

Toni nods affirmatively.

TONI

This isn't official though. See, one of the owners is going through a nasty divorce. His wife is trying to take him to the cleaners, with a double rinse thrown in. Well, his partners in this business aren't anxious to run the company with her calling the shots. That led

(CONTINUED)

(MORE)

to fighting in the executive suite. To complicate matters, we're getting our asses kicked in the marketplace by Awesome Beverages, which is owned by food giant Major Brands. Major Brands has deep pockets, so they're outspending us in advertising. Our market share has been declining the past eight months.

NICK

The new graphics could give you the marketing shot you need. Give me a chance. Let us develop the graphics for you on spec. There won't be any obligation on your part. But if you should decide to go with preprinted boxes, we'll be ready with the artwork out of the way.

TONI

Okay, okay. You sold me. But I don't think I can sell the owners, not with the way they're fighting.

NICK

Not to worry. I'll have the artwork in a week just in case.

INT. ROCK BOX OFFICE - DAY

• • •

Nick is speaking to a graphic artist. He's holding a reduced size billboard ad for Icy Teas.

NICK

You all set on the concept?

ARTIST

Yeah, all set. Give me a week.

NICK

Thanks.

EXT. FARM SETTING - DAY

Nick pulls up to a farm house.

INT. GREENHOUSE - DAY

Nick walks up to a very elderly man.

NICK

Mr. Fisher?

It's apparent that Mr. Fisher is hard of hearing, as he has to lean forward to hear Nick.

MR. FISHER

Yup, that's me.

NICK

Mr. Fisher, my name is Nick Williams with Rock Box. I understand you purchase boxes for your produce?

MR. FISHER

Yes, I do. Come into my office.

INT. MR. FISHER'S OFFICE - DAY

. . .

Mr. Fisher's office is tiny. A small desk and two chairs is all that can fit in the room. Mr. Fisher reclines his chair against the wall as he speaks to Nick, who is seated four feet in front of him. A clock radio sits on a shelf, above Mr. Fisher's head. The radio is playing head banger hard rock music at a very loud level. Mr. Fisher is talking, Nick is leaning in toward Mr. Fisher, but still can't hear a word he's saying.

EXT. FARM HOUSE - DAY

Mr. Fisher walks Nick back to his car.

MR. FISHER

Sorry that I can't help you. As I told you, I buy my boxes from a lifelong friend, but it was great talking to you.

NICK

Likewise.

• • •

Nick rolls his eyes upward.

MR. FISHER

There is a farmer down the street that uses boxes. Cardoza Farms. Ask for John Cardoza and tell him I sent you.

NICK

Thanks for the lead.

Nick gets into his car. He can't pull away from Fisher's Farm fast enough. Nick shakes his head and wiggles a finger in his ear as he drives away, trying to clear his ears from the loud music he was just exposed to.

EXT. ROADSIDE FARM HOUSE - DAY

Nick pulls into the yard of Cardoza Farms. The barn doors are open, yet there's no sign of life.

Nick gets out of his car and walks toward the barn. Nick starts to call out for someone.

NICK

Hello, Hello?

Suddenly, from inside the barn two German Shepherds appear. The dogs start barking and growling. Nick starts to back up, step by step. As soon as he senses the car's presence behind him, he turns, jumps in and slams the door. The two dogs jump up against the driver's side window. They are barking and growling as they scratch against the window. Nick starts the car and peels out of the yard in reverse.

INT. ICY TEAS OFFICE - DAY

Nick and Toni are both studying the artwork that Nick has submitted.

TONI

This looks terrific. I'm really pleased with it. I showed it to the owners this morning and they also liked it. Unfortunately, they danced around any commitments because of what's going on behind the scenes. Like I don't know what's happening. They told me to thank you for the effort, and they'll be getting back to us if they decide to proceed.

NICK

That's just what we expected, and that's okay. But if and when they decide to go with it, we're ready.

INT. ROCK BOX OFFICE - DAY

Nick is sitting at a desk in the sales office. The four color artwork for Icy Teas is sitting on the desk. Edward enters the room and notices the artwork on the desk. He approaches Nick.

EDWARD

Hey. That artwork looks great. Has Icy Teas seen it?

NICK

They all saw it this morning.

EDWARD

Well?

NICK

They really liked it.

EDWARD

And?

NICK

They're thinking about it.

EDWARD

What's there to think about? Just close the deal. You took it this far. Take it all the way. I expect an order from you soon.

NICK

But...

Edward cuts Nick off.

EDWARD

No buts. Just results. (Pause)

NICK

But...

Again Edward interrupts, this time putting his finger in the air to silence Nick.

EDWARD

Call them again.

NICK

I just spoke to them this morning.

EDWARD

All the reason to call them again. I'm going back to my office. Let me know.

Edward leaves the sales office. Nick shakes his head, then grabs the phone and dials.

NICK

Toni please..thanks. (Pause)

Hi, Toni. It's me again. Sorry to bug you but my boss is asking if there's any possibility of you ordering the pre-print boxes?

TONI (V.O.)

There's a chance. If the partners work out their differences, you'll no doubt see an order.

NICK

Great. That's just what I needed to hear. Thanks Toni.

TONI (V.O.)

You're welcome. Bye.

Nick hangs up the phone and heads for the door.

INT. THRESHOLD - EDWARD MOSS'S OFFICE - DAY

Nick walks past Ann, who sits outside Edward's office. Nick knocks on Edward's open door. Edward looks up from his work.

EDWARD

Come in.

Nick steps over the doors threshold.

EDWARD

Have you got the order?

NICK

No.

EDWARD

But you will? Right?

NICK

Uh, yeah. She told me the order is coming.

EDWARD

Did you tell her how much she has to commit to?

NICK

Yes. I covered it with her this morning. The order comes to seven hundred and fifty thousand dollars.

EDWARD

Good, because I'm going to forward the artwork to the mill tonight.

Nick looks stunned by Edward's comment.

NICK

Why?

EDWARD

Just to get the wheels rolling.

NICK

What's the rush?

Edward hesitates as he contemplates his answer.

EDWARD

Well, uh, because I want to give them all the time they need. You know, prevent errors by giving them additional time.

Edward's insincerity comes through and Nick looks puzzled not understanding the motive.

EDWARD

The order is coming, right?

NICK

Yeah.

Nick nods his head affirmatively, yet his expression isn't as convincing. Edward turns away quickly and doesn't see Nick's expression. Nick turns and exits Edward's office. Edward goes to this phone and presses a button.

EDWARD

Hi. How are you today?

VOICE (V.O.)

Fine, and you?

EDWARD

Better than great. I've got the pre-print order for Icy Teas and I'm Fed-Exing it to the mill tonight.

VOICE (V.O.)

Congratulations! And you made the deadline for the bonus. I was starting to doubt that you'd make it. It's been weeks since we talked.

EDWARD

Well, you know the saying, good things are worth waiting for.

VOICE (V.O.)

What's the due date on the finished boxes?

Edward hesitates for a moment surprised by the question.

EDWARD

Oh, we've got time. Adequate time not to have to rush things. I'll have the printed paper rolls in with time to spare.

VOICE (V.O.)

Great. Great. You're going to be a shoe-in for my job when it's available. Well, I've gotta run. Congratulations again.

EDWARD

Thanks. Bye.

EXT. CITY STREET - DAY

Nick is driving his car with his customer, Dave, in the passenger side. The car pulls off the road, into the parking lot in front of the bank. Nick parks the car. Dave opens his door and once again struggles his immense body out of the car. A stack of bank books are in his hands.

INT. LIZZIE'S RESTAURANT - DAY

Nick and Dave walk into the restaurant. The waiter that served them last time recognizes them. The waiter shows Nick and Dave to a table. Dave chooses the long bench seat side of the table and shoehorns his extra large body between the bench and the table. Nick takes the chair across from Dave.

WAITER

Can I get you gentlemen a drink?

DAVE

I'll have a Bloody Mary.

NICK

I'll have the same.

WAITER

Coming right up.

The waiter writes the order on his pad and leaves.

DAVE

Did I tell you about the woman I was seeing in France during the war?

NICK

Uh, no. You didn't. You were in France?

DAVE

Yup. Right after the war ended, I met and dated the most beautiful woman you'd ever laid your eyes on. She had the biggest tits, too.

Nick looks a little disbelieving. He then looks beside Dave on the bench. An elderly lady is eating a bowl of soup at the table next to theirs. She's seated almost next to Dave. Nick looks to see if she's heard Dave's comments.

DAVE

She'd let me do anything to her.

Dave's eyes light up as he reminisces.

DAVE

I bet I could have even sodomized her.

Dave's expression turns mischievous. He raises his voice.

DAVE

She loved oral sex.

Nick looks at the elderly lady again for a reaction. She appears unfazed, sipping her soup.

DAVE

She'd go down on me and slurp, slurp. She loved it.

Dave is now beaming at the memories, still talking loudly.

DAVE

She claimed the protein in sperm was good for her complexion.

Nick is now squirming uncomfortably in his seat as he steals a glance at the elderly lady sitting next to Dave. She continues sipping her soup, but her complexion has definitely taken on a red hue.

DAVE

She did have a great complexion.

The waiter brings the two Bloody Mary's to the table. He also brings a tray with hot sauce, Worcestershire sauce, lemon, and horseradish on it, and places it next to Dave's glass.

INT. EDWARD MOSS'S OFFICE - DAY

Edward is sitting at his desk, working on a pile of papers. He gives off the appearance of someone over his head. The phone rings.

EDWARD

Hello.

VOICE (V.O.)

Hi.

Edward recognizes his boss's voice and he smiles.

EDWARD

How are you?

VOICE (V.O.)
(Abruptly)

How longs it been since you sent the order out for Icy Teas rolls of paper?

Edward thinks for a moment.

EDWARD

Around three or four weeks. The order actually should be finished by now.

VOICE (V.O.)

Then you haven't read the Wall Street Journal this morning?

EDWARD

No. I haven't got around to it yet.

VOICE (V.O.)

Well, let me save you some time by reading an article to you. Awesome Beverage, a division of Major Brands, has announced that they have purchased Icy Teas company. The three week negotiations between the companies was concluded yesterday. The Icy Teas name will cease to exist as the plant will be converted to running the Awesome Beverage line of products.

Edward's face turns ashen at what he's heard.

VOICE (V.O.)

What's this all about? You did get an order from them, didn't you?

• • •

Edward's expression worsens.

EDWARD

Uh, no. But Nick told me it was coming.

VOICE (V.O.)

I thought this was your account?

EDWARD

(Quickly) It is. I have Nick handling the routine things.

VOICE (V.O.)

I don't consider seven hundred and fifty thousand dollars worth of paper printed Icy Teas routine. Icy Teas is dead.

EDWARD

Let me look into this matter!

VOICE (V.O.)

You better have some good explanation!

EDWARD

I'll be back. Bye.

Edward quickly hangs up the line, looks up a phone number and nervously places the call.

EDWARD

Hello, Phil Kane please. OK. I'll hold.

Edward waits for Phil to answer.

EDWARD

Hello, Phil. Hi. This is Edward Moss. Can you give me a status on my order for Icy Teas...Oh shit..It's all run? Oh, fuck...No, never mind. When was it shipped?..Oh, shit. Okay. Bye.

Edward is sweating like a marathon runner. He jumps up from his desk and heads for the door.

INT. ROCK BOX OFFICE HALLWAY - DAY

Edward Moss is heading down the hall in a frenzied stride. His agitation is apparent. He arrives at the sales office.

INT. SALES OFFICE - DAY

Nick is sitting at a desk, talking on the phone. Edward storms in and pushes the button on the phone, disconnecting Nick's call.

EDWARD

Where the hell is the Icy Tea order?

NICK

I'm still waiting. They told me they'd mail it when they're ready.

Edward is now nearly incoherent.

EDWARD

Ready? I've got three quarters of a million dollars in paper heading here by rail.

NICK

I told you I'm waiting for the order.

Edward finally erupts.

EDWARD

You'll answer for this.

NICK

What did I do?

• • •

Edward stands stunned, recognizing what Nick says is correct. He didn't do anything wrong. Edward looks like someone who's world is falling down around him.

INT. ROCK BOX CORRIDOR - DAY

Nick walks up the corridor toward Edward's office. He acknowledges Edward's secretary outside Edward's office.

NICK

Good morning, Ann.

ANN

Good morning.

Nick walks to Edward's office threshold. Nick knocks on the open door.

VOICE

Come in.

INT. EDWARD'S OFFICE - DAY

Nick walks in. Bob Wish is sitting at Edward's desk.

NICK

Well, how's it feel?

BOB

Pretty good. This poetic justice thing is pretty nice. Edward's chair is uncomfortable though. But hey, I'm the General Manager now. I'll just buy a new one.

NICK

I was so happy to hear they offered you his job. You deserve it.

BOB

Thanks. I never thought I'd see the day.

NICK

Did they tell you what became of him?

BOB

Yeah. They offered him a mandatory lateral transfer, which reads demotion. They gave him a job at corporate. The biggest thing he can fuck up now is an order of copy paper.

Nick and Bob laugh together at the thought.

BOB

We'll never have to deal with him again. Good riddance.

NICK

Amen.

BOB

There's one thing that I've been wondering about though. Did you know that Icy Teas wasn't going to be placing that order?

Nick shrugs his shoulders, exhibiting a funny, questioning expression. Bob doesn't know what to make of Nick's expression. He looks at Nick, trying to read him. He finally abandons the probe.

BOB

Well, get going. Don't you have boxes to sell?

NICK

Sure do.

Nick turns around and heads for the door.

BOB

Oh, one more thing.

Nick stops and turns around.

BOB

You might want to stop and tend to unfinished business in accounting on your way out. I've decided to do away with the no fraternization rule.

Bob smiles at Nick, knowing his comment would elicit a grin. Nick smiles back.

INT. ROCK BOX CORRIDOR - DAY

Nick walks down to the accountants office. He stops at Bonnie's doorway.

INT. BONNIE'S OFFICE-DAY

. . .

Bonnie looks up to see Nick.

NICK

Hi.

Bonnie and Nick's eyes meet. They both smile as they feel the chemistry between them.

NICK
(V.O.)

So, that was how happiness

and success manifested itself in my life. Things only got better as time went on. Employee working conditions and job satisfaction improved tremendously under Bob's management. The plant set productivity and earnings records that were unattainable under Edward Moss. Years later, Bob took an early retirement.

He's kicking back in the Caribbean last time I checked. I was promoted into his position, so now I'm running the plant. Oh, before I forget. Bonnie. Well, I'd like to say we got married and had kids, but we didn't. It may have felt right, but it didn't work out, just like she said. Sometimes happiness can happen without a fairy tale ending.

THE END

Images

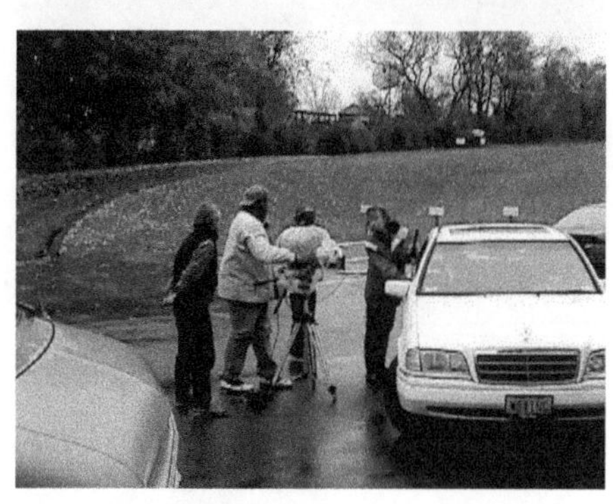

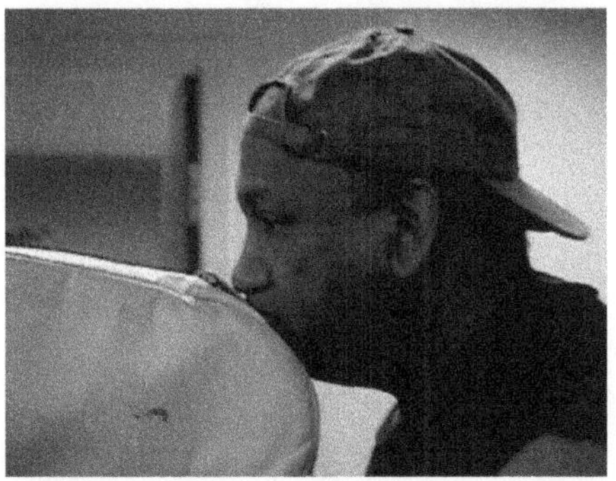

ACE BOX
CORPORATION

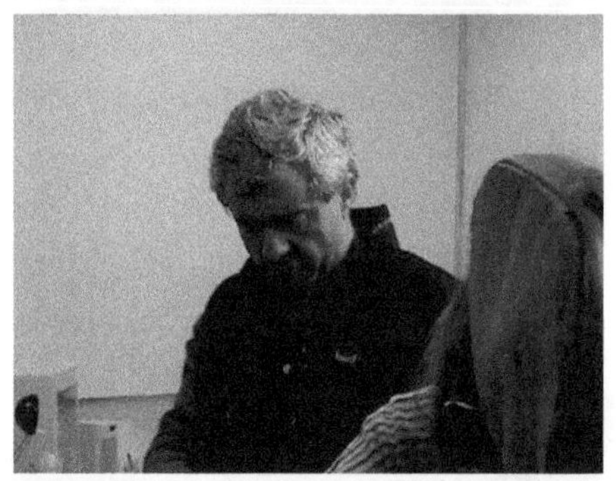

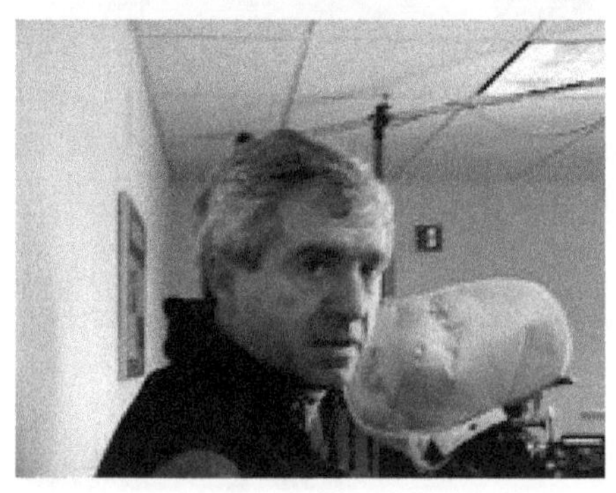

TRYING HIS HAND AT FILMMAKING is Nick Fasyanos (left), a wedding photographer and sales representative who recently wrote and directed a feature-length film entitled "Boxed Man." Pictured with Nick is Guy Weston, who as available part-time to help Nick with the shooting of his film. (Observer photo by Albert Tavakalov)

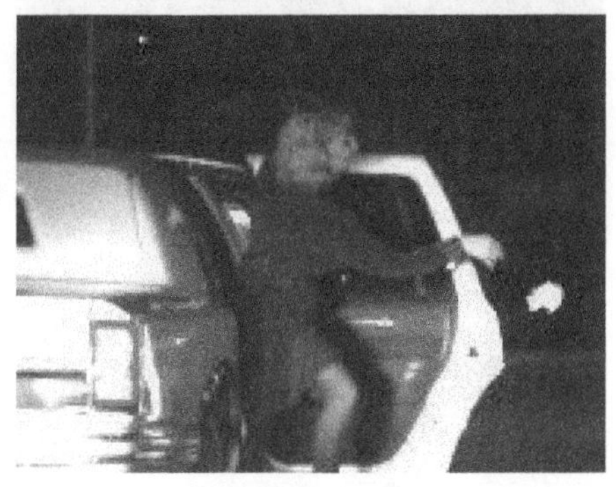

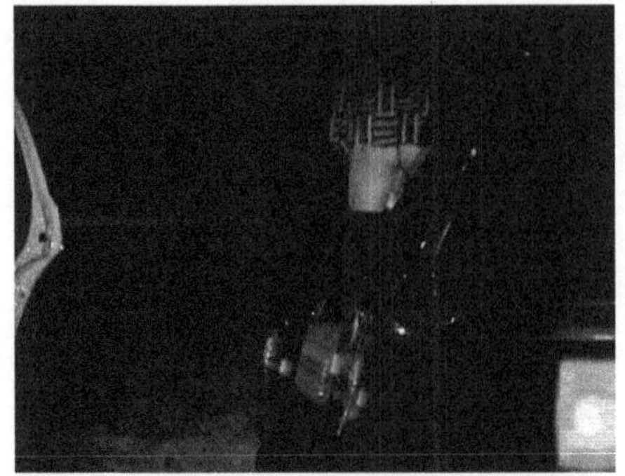

BOXMAN

AUX

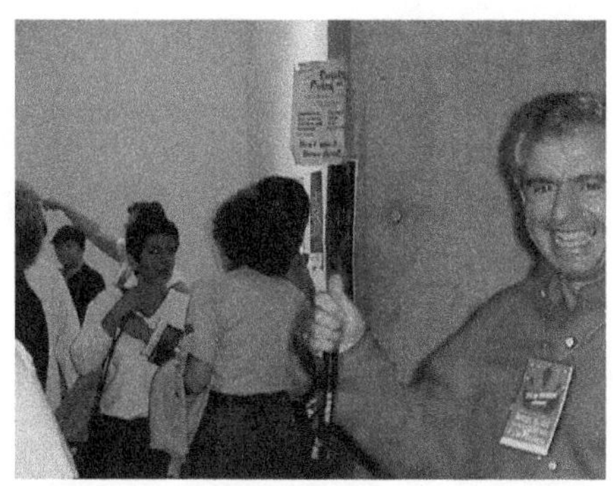

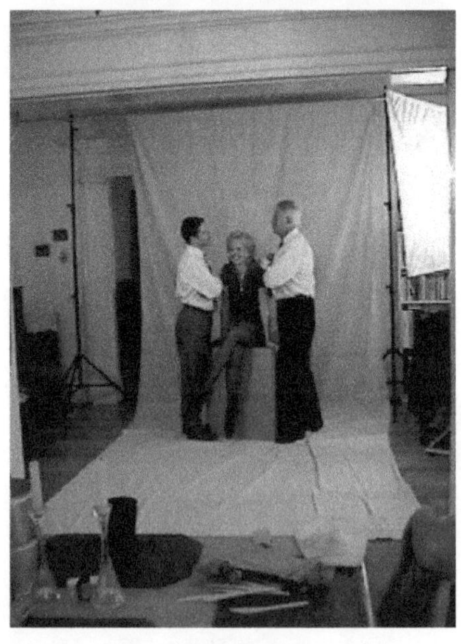

BOXMAN

BOXMAN
The Final Cut

EAST BAY

SERVING BARRINGTON, BRISTOL, LITTLE COMPTON, MIDDLETOWN, NEWPORT, PORTSMOUTH, TIVERT

WAITING FOR HIS BIG BREAK.

You'll laugh, you'll cry

Nick Pasyanos gives a thumbs up to filmmaking, a thumbs down for finding a distributor

'I feel like I almost got to the finish line, and I'm just dangling there.'

NICK PASYANOS

Parents urge Barrington to expand school music program

Newport Live

R.E. Reimer

Box salesman has smash hit at film festival

Hats off to Nick Pasyanos.

The Middletown filmmaker pulled down top honors in the Home Grown category at the just-ended Rhode Island International Film Festival, spread out between Woonsocket and Providence.

Pasyanos premiered his film "Boxed Man" before an overflow crowd at the Museum of Work and Culture in Woonsocket. The film won the "Best of Fest" award, determined by audience vote.

The 40-year-old box salesman made "Boxed Man" during free time on weekends. Friends and part-time actors and lots of careful planning were needed to tell the story of a frustrated salesman of boxes — based in part on Pasyanos' experience.

The comedy traces the salesman's adventures — and misadventures — through life and love.

Pasyanos had hoped to have the film premiere at the inaugural Newport International Film Festival this past June. But he needed about [illegible] to complete a print of the film.

That print wasn't done to make the Newport fest, but "Boxed Man" did make the Woonsocket festival — and won.

Now it's a matter of waiting to see if a distributor wants to push Pasyanos' comedy.

• • •

BUECHNER AT ARNOLD ART

A Director is Born

Local filmmaker gets his big-screen debut next week when *"Box Man"* premieres at the Rhode Island Film Festival

AVID FOR MOVIES

It's always showtime for film editor and technical pioneer Tom Ohanian of Cranston

Nick Pasyanos: The Rebirth of a Salesman

By Effie Lascarides

Special to The National Herald

PROVIDENCE, R.I.- Have you ever wondered what your life may have been like if you had pursued a different career? Did it ever occur to you that it might not be too late? Soon you'll be able to read an inspirational book by someone who did just that... but that will be when Nick Pasyanos finds the time to complete it. Right now he's too busy juggling three careers: that of a salesman and a portrait photographer for almost three decades and, recently, a filmmaker.

His most recent career started three years ago when he penned the script for a movie with the intention to try to sell it. That was his original goal. He fully recognized that one of the toughest challenges was trying to get into the Hollywood system "because they say that half the people in Los Angeles are walking around with scripts under their arms... I wouldn't doubt it! But I had to start somewhere... I love movies, I want to be in the business so I started writing some scripts. [When] I wrote a script that I really liked, [and] thought was marketable, I started compiling the names of people to start sending the script out to."

But two things changed his course. "Within a 12-hour period I saw a couple of small-budget films that clicked with me. All of a sudden I got the brainstorm that I wasn't going to sell the script. I was going to make the movie myself!"

As vividly as if it were today he remembers that he was driving on Route 195 when all of a sudden "the light bulb went off" in his head!

"I called my girlfriend from the car and told her: I'm making the movie! She thought I got into a car accident and hit my head! I said: No, no, no! I'm of sound mind and body. I'm going to do it!" He was so motivated that nothing could stand in his way; not even the approximately 60 locations or the many characters of the script.

Aware that he needed to educate himself in all aspects of filmmaking he allowed one year for preparation. He started devouring books about film, essentially living at book stores, and buying up every book that he felt could benefit him. At the same time

■ continued on page 3

section of The Observer and The North Providence North Star

First Take

Nick Pasyanos has spent many weekends in the North County area, shooting his first movie

'I found this whole other world while making this movie.'

lifebeat

Box man turns movie-maker

Candles key to soul survival

More filming in Valley, but not Corrente this time

'My whole philosophy was: Be prepared as hell. Every minute that camera is running it's $35.'

'Amistad' groupie turns inspiration into reality

Profile

■ ■ ■

NICK PASYANOS' 'BOXED MAN' — Nick Pasyanos of Middletown is the only local filmmaker featured in this weekend's second Rhode Island International Film Festival in Providence and Woonsocket.

The festival starts today and runs through Sunday with about 100 films featured. Pasyanos' film is "Boxed Man," a 110-minute feature about breaking into business in your 20s and seeing your ideals bump up against reality.

"Boxed Man" will premiere Sunday at 3:30 p.m. at the Museum of Work and Culture, River Island Park in Woonsocket. Ticekts are $6.

Pasyanos will also lead a forum Sunday at 1 p.m. called "Making & Selling a Movie in the 'Indie' World and the Hollywood Myth," at St. James Episcopal Church on Hamlet Avenue, Woonsocket. "Indie" is slang for independent films and their makers.

R.E. Reimer is a Daily News staff writer.

LIVING Saturday

DREAMS of a salesman

First-time filmmaker learns by watching pro at work on 'Amistad'

A

Dear reader,

We hope you enjoyed reading *BoxedMan*. Please take a moment to leave a review, even if it's a short one. Your opinion is important to us.

Discover more books by Nicholas Pasyanos at https://www.nextchapter.pub/authors/nicholas-pasyanos

Want to know when one of our books is free or discounted? Join the newsletter at http://eepurl.com/bqqB3H

Best regards,
Nicholas Pasyanos and the Next Chapter Team

CPSIA information can be obtained
at www.ICGtesting.com
Printed in the USA
LVHW032012101121
702935LV00002B/87